Collaborative Ministry:

Communion, Contention, Commitment

NORMAN P. COOPER

Paulist Press
New York · Mahwah

Book design by Nighthawk Design.

Library of Congress Cataloging-in-Publication Data

Cooper, Norman P., 1955–
    Collaborative ministry: communion, contention, commitment/by Norman P. Cooper.
      p. cm.
    Includes bibliographical references.
    ISBN 0-8091-3376-8
    1. Christian leadership—Catholic Church. 2. Lay ministry. 3. Cooperative ministry.
4. Catholic Church—Clergy. 5. Church renewal—Catholic Church. 6. Universal priesthood. I. Title.
    BX1920.C67 1993
    253′.08′822—dc20   92-38074
                                                    CIP

Published by Paulist Press
997 Macarthur Boulevard
Mahwah, NJ 07430

Printed and bound in the
United States of America

CONTENTS

COMMITMENT

Contents

To my parents,
Elizabeth and Dennis,
with love and gratitude
for teaching me what ministry is all about

ABBREVIATIONS

A.A.	*Apostolicam Actuositatem:* The Decree on the Apostolate of the Laity.
A.G.	*Ad Gentes:* The Decree on the Church's Missionary Activity.
Canon	The New Code of Canon Law, 1983.
C.D.	*Christus Dominus*: The Decree on the Pastoral Office of Bishops in the Church.
C.L.	*Christifideles Laici:* On the Vocation and the Mission of the Lay Faithful in the Church and in the World.
D.V.	*Dei Verbum*: The Dogmatic Constitution on Divine Revelation.
E.S.	Paul VI, *Ecclesiae Sanctae III:* Norms for Implementing the Decree on the Church's Missionary Activity.
G.S.	*Gaudium et Spes:* Pastoral Constitution on the Church in the Modern World.
L.G.	*Lumen Gentium:* The Dogmatic Constitution on the Church.
N.A.B.	New American Bible.
P.O.	*Presbyterorum Ordinis:* The Decree on the Ministry and Life of Priests.
R.C.I.A.	Rite of Christian Initiation of Adults.
S.C.	*Sacrosanctum Concilium:* The Constitution on the Sacred Liturgy.
S.D.	*Spiritus Domini:* Directory Concerning Ecumenical Matters: Part II, Ecumenism in Higher Education.
T.I.	Karl Rahner *Theological Investigations,* 20 vols. London: Darton Longman and Todd, 1961–84.
U.R.	*Unitatis Redintegratio:* The Decree on Ecumenism.
Vat II	Austin Flannery, ed. *Vatican Council II: The Conciliar and Post Conciliar Documents.* New York: Costello Publishing, 1987.

ACKNOWLEDGEMENTS

The integration of ecclesiological research with theological reflection and pastoral development contained in this book is itself the product of collaboration with mentors, colleagues, and friends. I am deeply grateful to Dr. John Ford, Dr. Peter Phan, and Dr. Richard DeLillio of The Catholic University of America for their professional counsel, support, and critical comments; Rev. Ryszard Holuka, Dr. Doug Morrison, and Dr. Carmen Nanko for their insight and friendship; Sue Knight and Susan Suprock for supervision in computer software skills, and careful manuscript editing; Leslie Ratzlaff for copy editing and critique; Doug Fisher and the staff at Paulist Press for professional guidance; and the members of the five parishes where I have ministered for their formative influence, remembering in particular the ordained and lay ministers of Blessed Sacrament Catholic Community, Alexandria, VA, for their witness to collaborative ministry.

PREFACE

About twenty thousand lay people and religious have become part of parish staffs throughout the country. This is in addition to all those who serve on parish school faculties. It is also in addition to the thousands upon thousands of parishioners who give their time to the various works and activities of their parishes, serving as lectors or eucharistic ministers, cantors or choir members, organists or other musicians; as catechists and in programs for the young people; in service to the elderly, the poor, or the bereaved; as members of community organizations working to correct injustices and to ensure better quality of life in the community; or in a host of other efforts to care for one another and to enable the community of faith to worship and work at the task of being disciples of Jesus in the community of the church and the arenas of the world. For discipleship that is not carried into family, work, and world is no discipleship indeed.

The parish then remains a remarkably resilient community, a structure that can embrace any concern and respond to any change. It is perhaps not the variety of activities found in American parishes that distinguishes the present from past generations. It is rather in the posture and style of parish ministry that today's parish life is distinct and challenging. By posture, I am referring to the extraordinary inclusiveness of parish life, the hospitality and concern extended by parish schools, programs for the elderly, social ministry and other programs to all in need, almost irrespective of the nature of their relationship to the worshiping community. By style, I mean that new kind of shared responsibility and cooperation that exists between the clergy and the laity.

At the level of ministry, this new style is perhaps best expressed by the catechumenate, the rite for welcoming adults into the church, responsibility for which is shared by the entire parish community and the result of which is to be not only admission to the sacraments but expectation that the new member will take on some responsibility for serving others in the community. At the level of leadership, the new style is best expressed in parish pastoral and finance councils and in parish staffing structures. The councils represent a desire for parishioners to share with their pastors and staffs responsibility for determining priorities, adopting appropriate practices, and exercising good stewardship regarding all the spiritual and material gifts the parish possesses. The staff structures—role descriptions, staff meetings, shared prayer and planning, good personnel procedures for hiring, supervising, and evaluating—represent an effort to combine the abilities of the pastors and staffs for the best enablement of the whole parish to exercise its responsibility to its members and to the mission of the gospel in the world.

What is remarkable, from the studies of the National Pastoral Life Center, is how much has been accomplished by pastors, the new staff members, and parishioners to adopt this new posture and style of church life.

It is this new style of church—a new ecclesiology, spirituality, and organizational pattern—that Norman Cooper addresses in this book. The new style is, as he describes, a new way of thinking (Pope John Paul II used the expression, *novus habitus mentis*), of feeling (the pope writes in his recent document on clergy formation about a relational disposition as essential to parish life), and of acting (carrying out the conviction that all are called to share their gifts for the good of the church). Consequently, his scheme for the book, and for a workshop that will promote this way of being parish, begins with ecclesiology and spirituality, and works through leadership styles and planning processes to help parishes live out this new style. With a bit more tendency than I would share to contrast the clergy as resistant and the laity as properly disposed to this new way of life, the chapters put a premium on being self-reflective and quite intentional about how all can work together and decide the future of their relationships and their ministries for the good of the parish. Such reflectiveness and intentionality, for which procedures are available, are essential for the future and must challenge the assumption often held by members of any institution that there is little room for initiative, little opportunity to shape one's own future.

Father Cooper combines homely anecdotes from his personal experience and from his travels throughout the United States and Italy with organizational perspectives that raise the incidental to the level of the thematic and happenstance to the level of the systematic. The catetgories he chooses—ecclesiology, spirituality, leadership style, parish mission statement, and pastoral planning —are helpful to any parish that wishes to review and redirect its efforts to achieve greater consistency and effectiveness.

Philip J. Murnion

INTRODUCTION

Collaborative ministry is rooted in the understanding of the church as communion, in which all the people of God participate in the universal call to holiness, mission, and ministry. Collaborative ministry calls all the baptized to a communal expression of their priestly, prophetic, and royal ministry, to utilize their gifts in building up the ecclesial community, to mutual respect, and to participate in dialogue. Collaborative ministry can empower the church to be more effective in its mission, yet it is seldom initiated within the context of a reflective process that combines an understanding of the ecclesiological, spiritual, and interpersonal dimensions of collaboration with a pastoral plan of implementation. Members of the same parish pastoral team often have vastly different understandings of the ecclesiological, spiritual, and interpersonal dimensions of collaboration. There is a need for a theological foundation that promotes the development of collaborative ministry.

This book explores six issues: (1) an ecclesiological foundation for collaborative ministry; (2) a spirituality that underpins collaborative ministry; (3) leadership styles that facilitate collaborative ministry; (4) an integration of the ecclesiological, spiritual, and interpersonal components of collaborative ministry with a parish mission statement; (5) a process for strategic pastoral planning; (6) a workshop that refines a diversity of skills necessary for collaborative ministry.

Chapter I outlines the ecclesiological vision of Vatican II. Ministry is seen as a responsibility flowing from baptism. The whole church is called to assume responsibility for mission and ministry. Collaborative forms of ministry flow from the relationship between the common and ordained priesthood. The image of the church as people of God and the church as communion bridges the gap between a church in which only a few are the custodians of power and truth, and a church where all are responsible as active participants in the mission of

Christ. The church by its nature is communion and as such needs participation and co-responsibility at all of its levels. Such an ecclesiological perspective provides a foundation for collaboration in ministry.

Chapter II focuses on the call of the whole church to holiness. Each person has equal dignity, is capable of self-transcendence, and experiences Christ's presence when gathered in his name (Mt 18:20). Responding to God's word and utilizing the gifts received from Christ creates communion within the community. This chapter investigates diverse ways in which Christ forms community, calls all to be active in building up the kingdom, and instills in his church a sense of collegiality and communion. The exercise of spiritual leadership that facilitates the presence of Christ within the community is examined. The holiness of all is generated by the presence of Christ in the midst of every pastoral endeavor. The spiritual foundation of the community, necessary to empower all to fulfill their call as disciples of Christ, is explored. These components foster cooperation, nurture communion, provide a foundation for collaboration in ministry, and facilitate its further development.

Chapter III describes the transition from a church in which people are passive recipients of God's word and sacraments to a church that is responsible for the formation and growth of the people of God. Parishes look beyond traditional forms of ministry with a view to gathering the community in closer union with Christ, utilizing the resources of the faith community, and promoting belief in Christ in the wider community. Many manifestations of communion and collaboration have sprung up in parishes since Vatican II, e.g. the growth of ministries using the time and talent of individuals in liturgy, music, education, and leadership, pastoral and sacramental activity. The leadership styles that promote communion and collaboration within the parish pastoral team are examined and evaluated. The features that promote cooperation, foster communion, and develop collaborative ministry are investigated e.g. mutual support, supervision, feedback, and evaluation.

Chapter IV explores how collaborative ministry empowers the church to be more effective in its mission. A reflective process that combines an understanding of the ecclesiological, spiritual, and interpersonal dimensions of collaborative ministry with a pastoral plan of action adds to the overall effectiveness of a parish team. However, each member of a parish staff has an individual perception of the ecclesiological, spiritual, and interpersonal dimensions of collaboration in a pastoral context. A process integrating these concepts with a pastoral plan of action is needed if a group is to be effective as a pastoral team. This chapter provides a collaborative process for developing or reviewing a parish mission statement, a formula for spiritual development, and a discernment process for evaluating the mission statement. All the baptized are called to utilize their gifts in the consultative process of developing or reviewing the mission statement. When all are active in service, communion is experienced and community grows.

Chapter V examines how an ecclesiological and spiritual foundation for collaborative ministry can be integrated with a leadership style that sustains collaborative ministry and a strategic planning process that promotes collaborative ministry. This chapter focuses on: the consequences of the strategic planning process, the role of the planning committee, the importance of developing a mission statement, the methods of operation, the development of performance indicators, the monitoring of the implementation, the evaluation of the strategic planning process, and the role of scheduling in forward planning. The strategic planning process enables a diocese or a parish to do more than plan for its future; it enables a diocese or a parish to create its future.

Chapter VI identifies the goal, format, rationale, methodology, and preparation necessary to implement the workshop, "Developing Collaborative Ministry Within the Parish." The workshop promotes the call of all the baptized to a communal expression of their priestly, prophetic, and royal ministry, to a use of their gifts in building up the ecclesial community, to mutual respect, and to participation in dialogue. The workshop utilizes a reflective process that is designed to promote collaboration between ordained ministers and lay ministers. This process can be utilized by all engaged in ministry to promote cooperation, deepen communion, and enable the church to be more effective in its mission. The workshop provides a model for ecclesial development. This model contains a strategy for revitalizing the parish involving all ordained ministers, lay ministers, and those in formation for ministry, and a procedure that enhances faith formation, improves interpersonal skills, identifies sources of conflict and confrontation, and supervises the ongoing progress, planning, and development of collaborative ministry within a diocese.

Each chapter contains a combination of pastoral theology, critical incidents in ministry, and reflection questions which integrates the reader's consciousness of the nature of ministry with the essential skills for collaboration between lay, religious, and ordained ministers by providing material for study, discussion, theological reflection, spiritual growth, and pastoral development. The appendices provide material that can be used for implementing a workshop that promotes collaborative ministry. Where stories or examples are used to illustrate the text, careful attention has been paid to maintain confidentiality and anonymity through changing any identifying circumstances.

CHAPTER I

An Ecclesiological Foundation for Collaborative Ministry

An external consultant exploring the phenomenon of "priestless parishes" interviewed a priest who exercised the function of "sacramental minister" in two priestless parishes. The meeting began with the priest expressing anger at his job description: he stated that the parishes were neither *priestless,* nor was he merely a *sacramental minister.* His ministry involved being a member of two parish pastoral teams and both parish liturgy committees, and he also was held accountable to the two lay ministers who exercised the role of pastor in both parishes. The transition from being pastor for nine years in one parish to being parish chaplain exercising these various ministries in two different parishes was filled with stress. The diocese concerned had trained the "lay pastors" for their new responsibilities, yet had failed to address the priest's needs brought about by his change of role.

In earlier times it was easy to identify the respective roles of the priest, the religious, and the laity: the priest and religious received theological formation and exercised leadership in ministry, while the laity were not trained in the field of theology and received direction from the priests and religious. The past thirty years has witnessed a change in that trend. Currently, in the United States there are as many lay ministers studying theology as there are students for the priesthood, and lay ministry is respected as a professional discipline. Today there is a healthy sharing of responsibility between ordained and lay ministers for the mission of the church. Rather than emphasizing a leadership group, the church is called to further develop collaboration between ordained and lay ministers who exercise co-responsibility in building up the kingdom of God.[1] The church fulfills its mission to the world more effectively when it utilizes the resources of all its members.

Many lay ministers are committed to the call of serious spiritual development and theological investigation. They are conscious of their rights and duties in terms of ministry, e.g. to provide for the needs of the church, to participate in evangelization, and to promote social justice. They wish to be what they are called to be by virtue of their baptism: active, mature disciples of Christ. This new direction that the church is taking cries out for decentralization and broader ecclesial participation in church structures.[2]

During the past decade, parishes have experienced an explosion of diverse forms of collaboration between ordained and lay ministers. There are as many different definitions of collaborative ministry as there are pastoral teams attempting to develop the reality. Members of the same parish staff often have vastly different understandings of the ecclesiological, spiritual, and interpersonal dimensions of collaboration. What is needed is a comprehensive theological foundation that promotes the development of collaborative ministry.

This chapter focuses on: (1) defining collaborative ministry that promotes co-responsibility and shared decision-making, (2) identifying an ecclesial vision contained in the Second Vatican Council that sustains collaborative ministry, (3) equating a theology of ministry that integrates the vision of the church as communion with a clear definition of collaborative ministry, and (4) exploring the vocation of all the baptized to be active in mission and ministry.

What Is Collaboration?

Collaboration in ministry is a response to the call received in baptism and confirmation to recognize the Spirit's charisms in all. It is rooted in understanding the church as a communion of the people of God in which each member shares in the universal call to holiness, mission, and ministry. Collaboration is a way of acting more efficiently, and is a communal expression of all the baptized to participate in the priestly, prophetic, and kingly ministry of Christ. It requires mutual respect, is a sign of equality in faith, and calls all the baptized to seek the truth and serve the common good, confident that all have gifts to contribute to the mission and ministry of the church. This vision of shared ministry manifest in building up God's kingdom encourages attentiveness to the Spirit at work in others and demands an ongoing review of current developments. It implies availability to others, readiness to dialogue, and fidelity to build the ecclesial community together.[3]

From your own experience, can you identify several pastoral initiatives in which you feel your parish is practicing collaborative forms of ministry?

Working as a team engaged in ministry is far more demanding than many ordained and lay ministers realize. Within many pastoral teams there are several different operative visions of what the church is, which can create its own tension. This friction is further compounded when most ordained and lay ministers have traditionally been formed in isolation: ordained ministers in the seminary; lay ministers in diocesan institutes for formation. Frequently there are difficulties in communication.

For example, the pastor in one pastoral team I worked with expressed his deep disappointment that his pastoral team always canceled the staff meeting when he was unable to attend. In talking to him, I discovered that he had failed to outline his vision of the pastoral team when he hired each member of the staff, to express how staff meetings are designed to promote genuine collaboration in ministry, and to train team members to take responsibility for their ministry, yet he was deeply disappointed when the staff never gathered for meetings when he was absent. After four years the staff finally became more collaborative when they wrestled the facilitation of the staff meetings from the grip of the pastor, started rotating the responsibility for facilitating staff meetings, and introduced a process of evaluating the meetings. Despite the pastor's commitment to collaborative ministry, his failure to communicate his vision had actually hindered its development within the pastoral team.

Collaboration invites all the people of God to work together in ministry to build a shared vision of church. This means that no one person or group monopolizes the tasks, the initiatives, or the policy-making in the church. A new image of church is portrayed through collaboration in which the baptized work with others, empower each other, and utilize everyone's expertise.[4] Collaboration requires patience in sharing this vision of church and in working together in building up God's kingdom. Wisdom is necessary to discern what the Lord asks of each person, and courage is essential to challenge each other honestly. Full participation in decision-making is one fruit of collaboration that gives expression to our equal status through baptism.[5]

In your parish can you identify the ministries in which particular skills and expertise are effectively utilized to promote greater co-responsibility for building up the kingdom?

Collaboration can take place on the intellectual, organizational, and personal level, but demands trust, maturity, and commitment from those involved. In collaborative ministry leadership is exercised as service, yet the person in authority need not be the leader. Most leaders are conscious that when people's contributions are not invited or welcomed, participants do not dedicate themselves to the task at hand. Greater participation results in greater commitment.[6]

One parish I worked with experienced major difficulties with communication and consultation. A member of the staff worked with many leaders of the community for months preparing a parish event involving hundreds of participants. The organizing minister had neither informed the staff of the extensive consultation taking place in the parish, nor asked for their input. Consequently, the staff all felt that since their input in preparing the event was neither needed nor wanted, then their presence at the event was superfluous. When none of the other nine members of the staff attended the event, the organizer was deeply hurt by the lack of support from the rest of the staff. Ironically, the organizer was the one who continually spoke about the need for mutual respect and better communication among the pastoral team. Had the organizer consulted the other staff during the planning and development, all would have participated in the event.

Our baptism requires co-responsibility and a conversion to collaborative forms of administration. We are all called to trust others enough so that we can communicate honestly and freely, work together caringly, serve each other, be demanding of each other, tap each other's talents, and pray with each other.[7]

It is clear that collaboration in ministry is demanding and requires conversion, but the baptized cannot ignore the call they have been given. Collaboration is about forming an attitude of mind within the whole church to promote deeper communion among all the baptized. Evidence that such an attitude of mind exists should be seen in the practical organization and life of the church.

My experience is that the operational style used by many pastoral teams is fashioned on a business model in which the pastor is the chief executive officer, and each professional lay minister is a head of a particular department. Staff meetings consist of deciding the overall direction of parish development, setting goals and objectives for the respective ministries, and giving progress reports. Yet this managerial model is limited since it fails to effectively promote co-responsibility among the respective ministries for the mission of the church. A better organizational model is needed that respects the vision of the church and increases cooperation and shared responsibility among all for the mission of the church. The church needs to provide its own model that respects its tradition and gospel values, while engaged in a dialogue with society. Such a model can enrich one's personal appreciation and understanding of what collaboration means and can promote effective sharing of responsibility in building up the kingdom of God.

In what ways do your pastoral team meetings promote greater co-responsibility among all engaged in ministry? Can you suggest a process or a structure that will improve communication, utilize everyone's expertise, develop greater trust, and increase communion within the pastoral team?

An important challenge facing all ministers today is to define which vision of the church can sustain a collaborative model of ministry, and to work collectively to realize this vision.

The Church as Communion

The concept of communion is used in popular language and in a religious sense. Communion is used to describe the way individual subjects relate to one another: we communicate by gesture, sign, and language. Interpersonal communication enables us to identify the bonds that unite us with one another in which we experience a multitude of emotions and feelings. Our basic communion is further enhanced by family, cultural heritage, common language, and mutual love. When individuals share rituals, personal thoughts, and deep feelings, a bond of trust develops which creates a more profound communion. One of the most intense experiences of communion is manifest in close friendship and especially in marriage. Today we are more conscious of our communion with the environment and of our responsibility to preserve and develop it for future generations.

The secular understanding of communion is extended in religious language to include communication with the transcendent God. God is portrayed in the Old Testament in various anthropological descriptions, including powerful king, loving parent, considerate friend. Yet the various images highlight the distance that exists between God and humankind. The biblical concept of covenant that focuses on the relationship of loving attentiveness between gracious lord and subjects also highlights the distance between master and servant. The concept of *koinonia* or communion in the New Testament is significantly different. God's incarnation in Christ enables humankind to experience a more profound communion with God.[8]

Biblical studies reveal that *koinonia* or communion reflects a double relationship, one enriching the individual, and the other fostering church unity. Communion in the New Testament implies that Christians partake in Christ by receiving his Spirit and at the same time enter into a fellowship with each other in sharing different gifts. Communion in the Spirit leads believers to think alike, having the same love, being of the same mind or soul, seeking the one unity (Phil 2:1; cf. 1 Cor 1:9–10; 2 Cor 13:13). One manifestation of *koinonia* that expressed the individual's participation in the gift of the Spirit was the sharing of the individual's possessions (Acts 2:44–45; 4:32–37; 2 Cor 9:13; Rom 15:26–27; Heb 13:16). For St. Paul, sharing in the body and blood of

Christ in the eucharist came to be regarded as the special moment in the church's celebration of its unity. Communion is a gift received from God which enables all who share in this grace to discover a new bond that unites them (1 Jn 1:3–6).[9]

Its fundamental meaning speaks of the union with God brought about by Jesus Christ, in the Holy Spirit. "The opportunity for such communion is present in the Word of God and in the Sacraments."[10] Baptism and eucharist are the foundation, sign, and nourishment of the church as communion (1 Cor 10:16).

The ecclesiology of communion is a central and fundamental concept of Vatican II and has deep roots in human consciousness. The concept of *koinonia* or communion is rooted in the biblical understanding articulated by St. Paul to express the mystery of God's love made visible in Jesus Christ. *Koinonia* is one of many images used by St. Paul to express the most intimate union of humankind with God and with one another. St. Paul's use of *koinonia* may be compared to his image of the body of Christ and to his formulas about the Christian living "in Christ" and "with Christ." St. Paul proclaims, "It is no longer I who live, but Christ who lives in me; and the life I now live in the flesh I live by faith in the Son of God who loved me and gave himself for me" (Gal 2:20). This proclamation indicates a participation (*koinonia*) in the Spirit of God's Son (Gal 4:6). His usage resembles St. John's imagery of the vine and the branches (Jn 15:5,7) and John's concept of indwelling: the believer in Christ, and Christ in the believer (Jn 6:56). The communion shared between God and humankind expresses an intimate relationship and leads to the gradual divinization of humankind in Christ.[11]

When we respond to God's call to share responsibility and collaborate in building up the kingdom of God, we experience what it means to be in communion.

A formation community of ministers from twenty-four different nations that I lived with for a year in Italy had a profound effect on my ministry. The community was funded entirely by a communion of material goods. I recall fighting with myself about how much of my life savings to "put in common" with the community. Several people I consulted all told me to be cautious about the amount I gave. Their concern was: "If it doesn't work out and you leave after a few months, can you get your money back?" After many weeks of soul-searching I realized that I was placing my security in my bank balance and not trusting in God's providence. The decision to put my entire savings into the community was a liberating experience. The effects of sharing in a "communion of goods" were many: each member of the community enjoyed equal dignity, all were willing to share in a spiritual communion of goods, the church was experienced as universal and pluralistic, and the experience of communion was profound. A common experience of visitors to the center was that you could almost touch the risen Christ present among the community.

Can you identify significant experiences of communion in your personal experience? What expression of communion do you value most and how do you help to build it?

One image of the church that was developed at Vatican II and that promotes collaborative ministry is that of communion.[12] In a public address on the day following the conclusion of Vatican II, Paul VI stated: *Communio* speaks of the Christian's incorporation into the life of Christ, and the communication of that life of charity to the entire body of the faithful, in this world and in the next, union with Christ and in Christ, and union among Christians, in the church.[13]

Justice is not done to this concept of ecclesial communion when one simply understands it as a sociological or psychological reality. Communion stresses the vertical relationship with God as well as the horizontal sharing with other Christians. Moreover, the church understood as communion reveals the divine plan for the salvation of humankind.[14] The new people are united with Christ and among themselves by the gift of the Spirit, which all the baptized have received (Rom 6:4). The Spirit who proceeds from the Father and the Son and manifests the unity of the Trinity is also the same Spirit who throughout history is the constant source of communion in the church (Jl 3:1; Acts 2:17–21).[15]

The current cultural experience in the United States appears to contradict the in-built desire to build communion with God and union with others.

For example, one middle class parish that was actively promoting small faith-sharing groups throughout the parish discovered that it was fighting an uphill battle. People were invited to gather to pray over the scriptures, to promote gospel values in their relationships, and to cooperate with other groups for occasional liturgical celebrations. Many people rejected the invitation to belong to such faith-sharing groups since they did not want to give up what they prized highly, namely their independence. One parishioner summed up the attitude of many when he stated: "If I want to experience fellowship I go to my country club, bridge club, or social club, I don't want the church to provide me with an experience of communion." The greatest problem facing the parish organizers of such small faith-sharing communities was how to break down the barrier of individualism.

What forms of individualism can you identify in the interpersonal dynamics operative within your pastoral team that hinders the development of communion?

The church is by nature a communion in which all the baptized are called to participate and share responsibility. Vatican II urged a style of collaboration between the laity and clergy that produces a spirit of willingness and encourages lay persons to put themselves at the service of the church.[16] In Vatican II the vision of "church" is dominated by considerations of the interaction between the universal and the ministerial priesthood. Ministry flows from baptism and calls for co-responsibility. Such an ecclesiology provides a basis for expanding the laity's consciousness of ministry. It focuses attention on the essentials of the minister-priest role. In effect, many areas of service previously performed by ministerial priests, which are not specific to that calling, can now be performed by the laity, e.g. parish administration, chancellor and notary, and business manager of a diocese. The ministerial priest is able to put more time and energy into his proper tasks.[17]

What tasks do you feel your pastor currently addresses that would be better attended to by other ministers? How can you help him to relinquish these tasks and enable him to be more effective in ministry?

Greater collaboration between clergy and laity, working from a common vision of what the church is, is needed for the smooth running of the community and for its development. The mutual exchange of faith between ordained and lay ministers creates a deeper bond between them; thus lay leaders are able to exercise a mediating function between pastors and the community. This is evident in the laity's participation in diverse ministries within the community: in leading back those who have been alienated, in proclaiming the Word of God, particularly though catechetical instruction, and in offering their professional skills in pastoral care and parish administration. All these activities come together in the celebration of the liturgy (A.A. 10). Close cooperation between ordained and lay ministers in parish life should be part of our current experience. Mutuality in ministry is experienced when the laity make known to the pastor the current problems that people face in the journey of faith, and the laity are able to participate in the ministry of preaching the gospel to others. They, in their turn, benefit from the insights and ministry of the clergy.[18]

This is essential if the church is to be the sacrament of unity for the world and achieve the call to conversion, which leads to deeper mutual cooperation. Collaboration is the common vision, a truly Christian experience that is firmly based on the word of God and the teaching of Vatican II. To promote this vision of the church as communion, ordained and lay ministers need formation that furthers collaboration among all and the sharing of ecclesial responsibility.[19]

For example, one city provided a course of formation for ordained and lay ministers engaged in marriage preparation. Fifteen parishes participated, twelve pastors selected their best people and sent them for formation, and three pastors participated in the formation program together with their people. In all twelve parishes the pastor "sent his people"; not one of the teams trained in group preparation for the sacrament of marriage was used. This caused anxiety and frustration for all. Yet in the three parishes in which the pastor participated in the course together with his people, the skills of all the lay ministers were fully utilized in a marriage preparation program. When formation for ordained and lay ministers is integrated, communion grows and collaborative ministry matures.

Catholic ecclesiology possesses all the ingredients for unleashing "people power" in the church. The church calls all the baptized to identify and promote communion among the diverse ministries which builds up the kingdom of God. Cooperation between ordained and lay ministers who exercise coresponsibility for the mission of the church contributes to the development of a theology of ministry. We now explore the components of a theology of ministry that promote the development of communion.

Theology of Ministry

Since Vatican II, there has been a great deal of interest in ministry. The laity understand ministry today in ways that were unthinkable before Vatican II. They are convinced that everyone is called to service, they anticipate new directions in future ministries, and they seriously question the traditional clerical monopoly of ministry. Many laity currently involved in ministry enjoy service, find it rewarding, and see it as an expression of their own identity. As more people become full-time ministers with professional skills, there is a growing awareness that service is a necessary part of baptismal commitment in the church.[20]

But some lay ministers even with years of experience still see themselves as simply "helping hands" for professional staff, rather than ministers in their own right.

I had an interesting conversation with one of the facilitators of a parish Lenten retreat for the Rite of Christian Initiation of Adults. The lay minister had been active in the process for five years, matching each of the candidates with a suitable sponsor, planning the weekly formation sessions, and regularly providing input for living the word. Yet her perception of her role in the process astonished me when she stated, "I am just glad to help the director of the R.C.I.A. process in his ministry." This minister was extremely effective within the initiation process, yet failed to perceive she was engaged in "her own ministry," and not simply assisting the professional full-time minister in his. Much still needs to be done to educate lay ministers that they own their respective ministries and do not simply participate in the ministry of the ordained or the professional lay minister.

All who respond to the call of ministry are invited to a vocation of service that proclaims gospel values. Knowledge of the scriptures therefore is crucial as a source of prayer and piety and as a source and resource of ministry. A key characteristic of Christian ministry is that it is exercised in union with, and in the name of, the church. Living in union with the church is the first component of ministry, and those who exercise ministry in the church are aware of the complementary nature of other services. Since ministry portrays an understanding of the church, it is authenticated, and recognized by the church as contributing to the extension of the kingdom. Authentication involves evaluation and needs to be applied to all who minister. In this way, new models of ministry are able to emerge in response to current needs.[21]

What prevailing needs in your parish have called forth new models of ministry? In what ways are these models of ministry promoting communion?

Many ordained and lay ministers express the desire for an integrated program of formation that equips all to deal with expanding demands of the ministers' time, talents, and resources. Increased responsibility for ministry requires a dynamic formative process that stresses the unity between natural human development and the supernatural formation of the whole person. Since all ministry necessitates cooperation with others, there is need for teamwork and collaboration throughout the formation process.[22]

Professional lay ministers receive their formation either in university or in diocesan lay ministry institutes. Three common components in many lay ministry formation programs are: theological foundation, spiritual growth, and the development of personal skills. Yet most priests involved in lay ministry formation are engaged as instructors or facilitators. Today, priests need to be actively involved as participants in the formation process rather than as the experts providing the formation. In the past, priests and religious trained, formed, educated, and delegated responsibility to the laity. Today, formation, education, and the exercise of responsibility need to be the result of mutually beneficial interaction between priests, religious, and laity.

Many ministers called to provide pastoral care are conscious that people are looking for evidence of one's faith and personal commitment to God. A deeper knowledge of the faith is vital for all engaged in ministry to carry out the task of making known the message of Christ. The whole people of God are called to holiness by virtue of their baptism. What does this call involve for the individual and for the community?

Holiness is not a moral perfection achieved by human endeavor, but is the gratuitous gift of God. God alone is holy (1 Sam 2:2). We share in this holiness through Christ, who is our sanctification (1 Cor 1:30), and "of his fullness we have all had a share—love following upon love" (Jn 1:16).

All are called to holiness by God—called through the community of the church in which they experience the grace of God. The church is appointed to sanctify the people of God and takes its place with redeemed humankind sanctified by Christ. Through the sacraments the church sanctifies its members in Christ's name and is confirmed in holiness in this process.[23]

One encouraging sign in recent times has been the development of small faith-sharing communities in parishes. Most parishes have trained and competent lay ministers who promote "a spiritual communion of goods." Yet, my research in spirituality among ordained and lay ministers shows that the ordained ministers are less comfortable and least competent to engage in sharing personal experiences of living out God's word and sharing their own faith.

For example, during a residential retreat I had the task of leading a sharing group comprised of fourteen priests. All participants were asked to live out the phrase of the scriptures, "Whatever you do to the least of these my brothers, you do to me." The first session began with me sharing my experience of registration at 10:30 P.M. the previous evening. Having pre-booked to share a double room, I was ready to drop into bed when one of the organizers approached me to inform me of a crisis. A recently widowed father had just arrived together with his two teenage sons, and was demanding that he be given a double room in the center where I was booked. Unfortunately, he didn't accept that every single bed was taken in the center, and he threatened to walk out and drive five hours back home. I was extremely tired, yet felt that here was an opportunity to love "the least of my brothers" and give up my prized possession, my room. I ended up sleeping in the basement of a house that this family had been assigned—which slept not two people but twelve! When the other priests were invited to share their experiences of living out this phrase of scripture, the first gave an exegesis of the scriptural text, the second gave a reflection on the phrase, and the third gave a response to the previous priest's reflection. To enable the fourteen priests to share personal experiences of living out the phrase of the scriptures was like pulling teeth. Yet the forty groups of lay ministers participating in the retreat had no difficulty in sharing personal experiences of living that particular phrase of the gospel. Lay ministers have much to teach the ordained ministers regarding spirituality, faith sharing, and the call to holiness.

The social implications of Christian holiness are "the promotion of a more human way of life even in this earthly society" and the production of "an abundant harvest of good" (L.G. 39). Each member of the church comes to love God and neighbor with all his or her strength by following Christ in his obedience to God's will, which is the path to perfection. Christian life depends on the guidance of the Holy Spirit and the prompting of divine grace.

The sanctification of Christians is achieved through life and not on a road that runs parallel to ordinary life. It is "through their earthly activities" that Christians proclaim to everyone "the love with which God loved the world."[24] God's word of love is sown in the heart where it takes root, springs up, grows, and bears fruit. God's word evokes the response of prayer and reception of the sacraments, especially the eucharist. The fruits of union with Christ are the active service of the community and self-denial, which are demonstrations of the grace of God at work. A Christian is engaged in a dialogue of love in which all life becomes a means of sanctification.

All the baptized share the same vocation that invites commitment to mission and ministry and to spiritual and interpersonal formation. The pastoral experience of the past three decades manifests that many have responded to this call to active ministry and are collaborating in building up the kingdom. The cooperation and collaboration between the universal and ministerial priesthood in mutual forms of ministry has promoted communion. This increase in collaborative forms of ministry reflects the current experience of our society. Today, collaboration is valued and people are accustomed to expect it at home, at work, and in social and civic life. Businesses and political groups foster collaboration at all levels of their organizations. Research in managerial styles reveals that the greater the number of people consulted to identify needs, the higher the commitment from them to work at addressing these needs. Many businesses have abandoned a "top down" model of management in which a chosen few make the decisions and the employees carry out the work. Instead, the broadest base of employees are encouraged to participate in the planning process, which promotes greater sharing of responsibility for the future direction of the organization. We are currently witnessing the abandonment of old hierarchical structures in which a chosen elite exercise all the power, to more diverse and collaborative forms of organization in which a greater number of employees share power. This change poses certain problems for the church, since many clergy, though willing to sacrifice their status, lack the vision and skills to initiate collaboration with their lay colleagues.

The majority of ordained ministers are involved in parish ministry in which group work forms the basis for most experiences in ministry. Yet, my experience in facilitating workshops on collaborative ministry reveals that many were trained in the dynamics of one-on-one ministry and lack the necessary skills to engage effectively in group process that forms the foundation for collaborative ministry.

For example, the current pastoral requirements that candidates for the priesthood are expected to fulfill are very limited. One seminary I worked with asks candidates to complete three courses: Introduction to Pastoral Ministry, Clinical Pastoral Education, and Social Ministry. The mission statement of the seminary states they are training men who are "competent and skilled in collaborative forms of ministry." Yet there is no course on Pastoral Leadership or Group Process offered. How can seminarians identify and develop the necessary skills to be effective in collaborative ministry when the courses required to refine these skills are not currently offered. My concern is that we are currently training a new generation of clergy who have the right jargon, but lack the basic skills necessary for exercising effective leadership in the church. An urgent need is to provide all ordained ministers with a comprehensive formation program in group process that is inclusive of lay ministers.

The church promotes cooperation between ordained and lay ministers by providing formation for their ministry and mission in society. Such formation is diverse and needs to keep pace with the spiritual and doctrinal progress of the church and to be adapted to various circumstances of apostolic activity. Formation needs to be holistic and must take into account the gifts and circumstances of each individual. Since the ministry consists in fulfilling the mission of Christ and the church, it needs a spiritual foundation that enables the individual to see God, others, the world, sin, and salvation with the eyes of Christ.

What type of ongoing formation has been most valuable to you during this past year? How has it enriched your ministry? In what ways was it holistic?

Without collaboration, the church encounters serious difficulties in bringing Christ's call to modern men and women, since many are accustomed to consultation and sharing responsibility in decision-making in their work environments, and now expect similar treatment from the church. Effectiveness in ministry flows from a living experience of communion that manifests itself through collaboration. The 1985 Extraordinary Synod stressed the ecclesiology of communion as a central concept of Vatican II and saw collaboration as a concrete expression of this vision.[25]

The 1987 Synod of Bishops further explored the diverse ways in which the entire church is called to be active in ministry. What contribution did this synod make to our understanding of the church as communion and how did it promote collaborative ministry?

The Mission of the Laity

The 1987 Synod of Bishops, "On the Vocation and the Mission of the Lay Faithful in the Church and in the World," was preceded by extensive consultation between bishops and laity. The discernment process was collaborative in design and helped articulate the call of the universal priesthood of the people of God to mission and ministry. This extensive consultation fostered communion.

In his address to the synod, Archbishop Chiasson pointed out that baptism is the underlying theological foundation for any development or discussion of the notion of the church as communion.[26] Archbishop Hayes appealed for broader participation of the laity to ensure that the whole people of God have an active part "in dealing with the issues that directly concern the good of the entire Church."[27] This proposal expresses the church envisioned by Vatican II and strongly underlined in the 1985 extraordinary synod in its notion of the church as communion. Constant dialogue between church members and those responsible for ministries and services is necessary. In this way, co-responsibility, collegiality, and collaborative ministry can be realized.[28]

The 1971 Synod of Bishops on Justice in the World stated, "We also urge that women should have their own share of responsibility and participation in the community life of society and likewise of the Church."[29] This agenda is a significant challenge facing the church today and was taken up by the National Conference of Catholic Bishops (N.C.C.B.) in 1983 when they issued a first draft of a pastoral letter on the role of women in the church. The feedback from this pastoral shows the urgency of this issue since the credibility of the church in its pastoral mission is at stake. Women asked that they be treated as partners in finding the solutions to the church's mission in society and be treated openly, trustingly, and respectfully.[30] Women in the gospels ministered to, with, and for Jesus. He, in turn, was sensitive to their needs.[31] In 1988 the N.C.C.B. issued a response to women's concerns for church and society in the first draft of a pastoral letter that promoted co-discipleship and respect for the role and gifts of each person regardless of gender.[32]

The bishops respected the dignity of the person as being the most precious possession of an individual. Each person, created in the image and likeness of God, redeemed by the blood of Christ, is a living temple of the Spirit destined for eternal communion with God. The dignity of the person constitutes the foundation of the equality of all people and also is the inalienable right of every human being.[33]

Working with various pastoral teams, I discovered that eighty percent of lay ministers were competent qualified professional women. Yet pastors who were insensitive to women's issues often showed a lack of respect for the dignity of the women in their pastoral team, and failed to allocate resources for their professional development. When treated in this fashion, the dignity of women as equal partners in ministry is denied, and they are kept in a subservient role in their relationships with the pastor. My experience was that pastors shared in private their struggle of how to relate to professional women in ministry and not during staff meetings. A greater degree of openness and honesty is called for.

There is a real need for open dialogue between men and women engaged in parish ministry to identify and address the fundamental issues that deny women their God-given dignity.

Can you identify ways in which the dignity of all is not respected during your pastoral team meetings? What could you do to raise people's consciousness of the problem?

The synod fathers in 1987 affirmed the need to defend and promote the personal dignity and equality of women and recommended a fuller use of the diverse charisms of all the baptized in the mission of the church.[34] The rightful presence of women in the church and in society will be realized when a more perceptive and accurate consideration of the anthropological foundation for masculine and feminine attitudes is explored. The synod proposed the need to clarify woman's personal identity in relation to man: "The anthropological and theological foundations for resolving questions about the true significance and dignity of each sex require deeper study."[35]

All, by virtue of baptism and confirmation, share equally in the threefold mission of Jesus Christ, priest, prophet, and king. All are charged and given the ability to fulfill the fundamental ministry of the church: evangelization. John Paul II acknowledges the active and responsible presence of women in the church in theory, and he states that it must be realized in practice. In the exhortation *Christifideles Laici,* John Paul II persistently used inclusive language.[36] The revised Code of Canon Law contains many provisions on the participation of women in the life and mission of the church (Canons 204–05; 208; 229; 231; 327–29; 460–68; 492–94; 511–14; 517; 536; 1112; 1122). These provisions are to be made more commonly known and implemented with greater determination.[37]

Conducting workshops on collaborative ministry and researching pastoral planning in eleven dioceses in the U.S., I discovered that most women engaged in parish ministry and all the women responsible for diocesan offices have a firm grasp of group process. Yet many ordained ministers are limited in their understanding of the dynamics involved in group process. I believe that women will be perceived as equal partners in ministry when ordained ministers receive the necessary formation in group process and interpersonal development.

John Paul II urges the coordinated presence of both men and women in pastoral situations so that the participation of the lay faithful in the salvific mission of the church can be complete and harmonious.

One model of the coordinated presence of men and women active in ministry is manifest in a parish of seven hundred households. In 1981 I was instrumental in developing a communications group called the "Link Group," which consists of seventy parish visitors each responsible for ten households. The goals of the "Link Group" are: (1) to provide materials and information from the pastor to each household in the parish four times a year; (2) to identify and prioritize the pastoral needs in each household; (3) to be co-responsible with the pastor for addressing these needs; (4) to promote a deeper sense of belonging to the local church. A significant factor in the success of this communications ministry during the past ten years had been the coordinated presence of men and women representing the different age groups within the parish.

The unity of all states of life within the church and the living out of Christian dignity are an expression of the church as communion. They are different, yet complementary, and are placed at each other's service in the mission of the church: "While different in expression, they are deeply united in the Church's mystery of communion and are dynamically coordinated in its unique mission."[38]

The process used to prepare for the 1987 Synod on the Laity manifested a mutual respect for men and women engaged in ministry. The extensive consultation among all the baptized in preparation for this synod increased cooperation, promoted collaboration, and developed communion. The synod emphasized the need for: (1) broader co-responsibility and dialogue among all called to mission and ministry, (2) the education of all regarding the dignity and role of women in the church, and (3) the promotion of mutuality between men and women engaged in ministry. These significant concerns were explored during the preparation for and the celebration of the synod and promote the development of collaborative ministry.

Can you identify the ministries or programs in your parish that effectively promote the mutuality of women and men engaged in ministry? What more needs to be done to further promote this reality?

Summary

The ecclesial vision of Vatican II focusing on the church as communion affects all who participate in ministry. The whole church is called to assume responsibility for its mission and ministry. Where essential links exist between ordained and lay ministers, this promotes an increase in collaborative forms of ministry. Presently, laity have increased apostolic responsibility and are receiving formation through instruction in theology, ethics, and philosophy which enables them to exercise spiritual leadership within the community. When formation, education, and the exercise of responsibility flows from interaction between clergy and laity, the church is manifest as communion and gives witness to mutual participation and co-responsibility at all levels. Shared responsibility requires that every baptized Christian be guaranteed not only freedom to be responsibly involved in ministry, but also freedom of speech regarding what he or she judges to be the best for the church.

If the whole church is to assume responsibility for its mission and ministry, then the whole church ought to be involved in every level of decision-making, be that at the local or universal level. This need not mean one person one vote, but it does mean that more than lip service is paid to the notion of the *sensus fideles*.[39] The developments in lay ministry over the past three decades need to be viewed with a real sense of satisfaction and hope. There is evidence that cooperation and collaboration between ordained and lay ministers promotes deeper communion. This heralds a genuine reform and appears to mark a period of ecclesial reform.

The ecclesiology of communion promoted in Vatican II demonstrates the vision of what we are called to be as church.[40] No longer is the church a place in which only a few are the custodians of power and truth, but it is a dynamic reality in which all are responsible as active participants in the mission of Christ. The people of God is more a community of active people who use their charisms in diverse forms of ministry to promote cooperation, collaboration, and communion as they build up the kingdom. If the renewal of the church is to be experienced, fidelity to one's baptismal vocation is essential. Each person is to use all the appropriate means to preserve and develop this baptismal vocation: meditation on the word of God, prayer, spiritual reading, sharing of material and spiritual goods, and ongoing formation, plus a clearly defined involvement in ministry.

How can communion be realized within the church? A spiritual foundation for collaborative ministry outlines how to be church and explores how communion is fostered and developed. All the baptized are called to holiness, to utilize their gifts to build the kingdom of God, respect one another's dignity, and collaborate in ministry. A spiritual foundation for collaborative ministry promotes co-responsibility in ministry and builds communion in the parish.

The entire people of God need a spiritual formation that sustains collaborative forms of ministry and deepens communion within the church. What are the essential components of such a spiritual foundation? Do all the baptized share equal dignity? How can the gifts of all be utilized in ministry to build up communion? Who is responsible for the mission of the church? How can communion be developed in the parish and how can the parish generate communion within society?

Chapter II responds to these questions by providing a spiritual foundation for collaborative ministry, which promotes cooperation, facilitates collaboration, and develops communion among all the people of God.

Reflection

1. An intense experience I had of communion with the risen Lord was . . .
2. I felt profound communion with others during . . .
3. I foster communion in my ministry by . . .
4. I share my experiences of communion with God and fellowship with others through . . .

Suggested Reading

1. Daniel J. Harrington, "Paul and Collaborative Ministry," *New Theology Review* 3/1 (February 1990), pp. 62–71.

2. Michael A. Fahey, "Ecclesial Community as Communion," *The Church as Communion,* James H. Provost ed. (Washington, DC: Canon Law Society of America Permanent Seminar Studies 1, 1984), pp. 4–23.

3. Leonard Doohan, *Grass Roots Pastors: A Handbook for Career Lay Ministers.* San Francisco: Harper and Row, 1989.

CHAPTER II

A Spiritual Foundation for Collaborative Ministry

A parish pastoral team I worked with in Michigan wishing to further their spiritual development were given the daily opportunity to celebrate the eucharist at midday. At first everyone attended, but several weeks later only one or two gathered regularly for the celebration. The pastoral team reviewed the situation and decided instead to gather for midday prayer of the church. All members of the pastoral team were asked to preside and share a reflection on the scripture of the day. This proved to be more successful since everyone participated in faith-sharing and the exercise of spiritual leadership. A far greater number of the pastoral team and other parishioners gathered for midday prayer than previously assembled for the celebration of the eucharist. The pastoral team discovered that sharing responsibility for presiding at midday prayer has encouraged them to be more prayerful during staff meetings.

The Second Vatican Council provided the church with a wealth of insights regarding the laity's role within the church. The rapid expansion of professional lay ministry during the past three decades has promoted a deeper experience of communion within the church. Many ordained and lay ministers are actively promoting collaborative ministry within parishes, yet struggle to identify a spirituality with universal appeal that can sustain this form of ministry. This chapter focuses upon the spiritual writings of Chiara Lubich,[1] examines the spiritual components that facilitate collaboration between all members of the church, and demonstrates how Christ's presence among the community has consequences for collaboration in ministry.

A spirituality that underpins collaborative ministry needs to be integrated with the ecclesiology presented in Vatican II by focusing on: (1) the dignity of every person, (2) the discovery of Christ's presence in the community and the individual, (3) the shared responsibility for the mission of the church, (4) the work of God's Spirit that generates communion, (5) the communion created by living the word of God (Jn 17:21), and (6) the realization of communion through the celebration of the eucharist. The Lord's presence among his people empowers all the baptized in their mission to sanctify the world, which requires us to die to ourselves and rise anew with Christ. Living out and sharing God's word with Christ present among us creates community, and celebrating the eucharist deepens communion. This spiritual foundation produces greater co-operation, co-responsibility, and communion among the whole people of God.

The Gift of Dignity

Human dignity comes from God's creative purpose, according to the book of Genesis (Gen 1:26–27). The human capability to sustain a relationship with God is manifest in the age-old religious experience of humankind. The history of religion indicates the ingrained understanding that our God engages our whole being. Within the spectrum of religious expression, Christ lightens up our awareness and focuses us on our commitment to work for the kingdom and to be so linked to him that life disconnected from him is inconceivable. The gospel of John (Jn 15) and Irenaeus of Lyons (d. 200) used the image of the grafted branch drawing life from the root stock of Christ able to produce acceptable and superior fruit. Negatively, our God-given freedom can be exercised in a way that introduces disunity—sin either weakens our sense of God or fundamentally disrupts communion with God.

The creation of humankind in God's image indicates that the creator called into being creatures who would have a relationship with their maker. All other beings were created according to their kinds (Gen 1:25). Only human persons are created "in his image" (Gen 1:27). Human beings have a direct personal relationship with God that is integral to their nature. Genesis perceives human life as having meaning in the context of a wholistic relationship with God. Religion manifests our relationship with God and involves the whole of life. Humankind is capable of responding to God's will and building up the kingdom, yet also is prone to sin. Sin is unable to destroy God's image within us, but makes us less receptive or unreceptive to God's love. The coming of Jesus refocuses us on God's image. Irenaeus affirmed that it was necessary to be "grafted" into the word of God in order to live in the image and likeness of God.[2] Gregory of Nyssa (d. 395) maintained that God is the source of love and all share this characteristic with him. If love is lacking, then the image is altered.[3]

The scriptures and many of the fathers express the equal dignity of men and women before God as created in God's image, and thus their equal ability to communicate with God.[4] This equality was promoted by the 1987 Synod of Bishops when they recommended a fuller use of the diverse charisms of all the baptized in the mission of the church (L.G. 32).[5] The dignity of the person constitutes the foundation for the equality of all and forms the basis for cooperation in ministry in which the church is experienced as communion.

While conducting workshops on developing collaborative ministry within a parish I saw the mutual dignity of women and men engaged in full-time ministry promoted. Each pastoral team planned a diversity of prayer sessions in which women and men exercised the role of presider, leading the assembly in prayer, praise, proclamation, and petition. The lay ministers' exercise of liturgical presidency during morning and evening prayer, liturgy of the word, communion services, etc. has helped to promote the dignity of all. My experience has been that professional lay ministers are competent to lead liturgical gatherings and faith-sharing groups, and eager to provide the resources for others to participate in this form of spiritual leadership. Yet this form of spiritual leadership can be perceived as a threat by some ordained ministers.

What liturgical celebration have you experienced in your parish that has promoted the dignity of all? What was significant about these celebrations?

Christ's Presence in Humankind

The gospels put special emphasis on the presence of Jesus with his apostles (Mk 9:37; Mt 10:40; Lk 10:16; Jn 13:20). This presence of Jesus with his emissaries takes on greater meaning after his resurrection. They are incorporated into Christ, and by their words and actions make Christ present to others. Love of Christ directed toward the neediest of his followers is an expression of love for Christ himself (Mt 25:31–46).

The believer's incorporation into Christ's body, the church, is expressed by the Pauline phrase, to be "in Christ." The communitarian dimension of being "in Christ" flows from our union with Christ (Col 3:9–11). Because Christ has united us with himself, we are called to cooperate with him and our brothers and sisters, irrespective of all previous differences. Paul affirms the identification of the believer with Christ which has made us new (Gal 2:20). This implies a communion of life, dialogue, dynamism, and growth until "Christ be formed in you" (Gal 4:19). This communion expresses the cooperation of all in the mission of the church. The presence of the Spirit in the Christian and the presence of Christ are inseparably bound to one another. To have the Spirit signifies that one belongs to Christ.

The presence of the Spirit was manifest during the 1970s in an explosion of commitment from lay ministers actively engaged in expanding the church's involvement in social justice issues. Dioceses with vision employed professional lay ministers to provide resources and training to parishes that promoted greater consciousness of our common call to actively oppose unjust systems which do violence to individuals and societies. The love of Christ has helped overcome tensions between those engaged in compassionate outreach to all suffering from injustice and oppression.

For John, the indwelling of the Spirit means that the believer is in Christ and Christ is in the believer (Jn 6:56). John speaks of bonding between Christ and the individual in the image of the vine and the branches (Jn 15:5, 7). In the first letter of John, we are reminded that our responsiveness to God's initiatives can be measured by our love of him and our action for others. We mirror the reality of God's love but we do not control or merit it (1 Jn 3:23–24). This union with Christ promotes the recognition of each other's gifts, encourages their use in ministry, and empowers the sharing of responsibility.

St. John of the Cross (d. 1591) affirmed, "When one's love for a creature is purely spiritual and founded in God alone, then in the measure that it grows, love for God grows in one's soul as well."[6] Jesus gives pre-eminence to love for God (Mt 22:37). A Christian must do as God does: not wait to be loved, but be the first to love. John tells us that God loves us and states, "Beloved, if God has loved us so, we must have the same love for one another" (1 Jn 4:11). Christ wants our love for one another to move us to compassion, to give ourselves totally to our neighbor and receive him or her into our hearts (Lk 10:33). This mutual love bears witness that God is present among us encouraging the cooperation of all in building up the kingdom (Mt 18:20).

One compassionate parish community I was actively involved with for several years had many people engaged in social ministry. The basement of the temporary church was used to provide a night shelter for sixty people. Parishioners cooked meals, served the guests, engaged them in conversation, and attempted to alleviate their suffering. The compassion of the community was manifest in the design of the new church development which included a new night shelter for fifteen to twenty people whose aim is to rehabilitate the individual whenever possible. This ministry cuts across a wide spectrum of the parish community, and manifests an integrated commitment to provide hospitality, temporary accommodation, and hope for the future. Many active in caring for the homeless speak about how they have been enriched by their interaction with the street people and now respect their dignity.

Our dignity stems from our relationship with Christ. The Spirit sustains this dignity and promotes union with Christ and our brothers and sisters. The presence of the risen Lord in the midst of his people is essential for all our commitment to ministry. It is Christ who gathers and facilitates cooperation within the community and empowers all in ministry. Where Christ is present among two or more gathered in his name, communion is realized, and the kingdom of God is manifest. This is the foundation upon which collaborative ministry is built.

When have you experienced the presence of the risen Lord while actively engaged in ministry? What impact did it have on you at the time, and with whom have you shared this experience?

Shared Responsibility for the Mission of the Church

Christ's presence brings light, joy, and peace to those who are united in his name. Pastoral initiatives that are discerned with Christ present among those gathered in his name promote cooperation and shared decision-making. Those committed to implementing the goals that are communally agreed upon recognize the presence of Christ in ministry as the summit and source of collaboration in ministry.

What are the conditions for establishing the presence of Christ among us? The presence of Christ is not limited to his physical presence in history; he is also present in the midst of two or three who are gathered in his name (Mt 18:20), in the word, in the eucharist, and in our brothers and sisters. Theophylact, bishop of Bulgaria (c. eleventh century), commenting on Matthew 18:20, states, "He doesn't say I *shall* be, as if putting off or delaying his presence, but I *am,* that is, I am already present."[7] St. Athanasius (d. 373) applied Matthew 18:20 to those who are far from one another, yet spiritually united: no distance can separate us since the Lord binds us together.[8]

For St. Basil (d. 379), doing the will of God is required for having Christ in our midst.[9] For St. John Chrysostom (d. 407), loving our brother and sister out of love for Christ, loving them as Jesus did who gave his life for his enemies, promotes Christ's presence in our midst.[10] Theodore the Studite (d. 826) finds mutual love to be the foundation for having Christ in the midst of the community.[11] Some fathers saw these prerequisites for having Christ in the midst of the church as the vocation of the entire church. Christ present among people who are united in his name is a source of joy and resolves any dispute.[12] In these circumstances Christ is present and facilitates the ministry of those who are gathered in his name. Ministry flows from this presence, is sustained by Christ, and becomes effective through him.

My experience has been that when pastoral team members are conscious of these conditions for generating the presence of the risen Lord, their preparation for staff meetings is more proactive. Suggestions from pastoral teams to ensure that the Lord is always present during staff meetings have included: to pray before and after staff meetings, to be more present to the Lord who dwells in me, to be emotionally and spiritually as well as physically present, to be gentle in word and action when we hold each other accountable, and to be conscious that God is present especially when issues that engage us emotionally are discussed.

St. Peter Chrysologus (d. 450) holds that ministry is more effective when supported by intercessory prayer: "If two of you shall agree on earth about anything at all for which they ask, it shall be done for them. . . . Christ did not mention one thing or another, but he promised to do everything—whatever the united request desires."[13] Many pastoral teams discover that when they pray for each other's ministry during the week, interceding in an intentional way, this breaks down individualism and promotes a deeper experience of communion.

All ministers are called to cooperate and be co-responsible for promoting the presence of Christ among the community. With Christ's presence among the community, pastoral initiatives can be better discerned, priorities can be decided, and goals can be set. All the baptized share the responsibility for implementing the agreed task in ministry and are responsible for giving appropriate feedback and evaluation. In this way, Christ is operative within every pastoral initiative, drawing all into communion with him and with each other.

Vatican II highlights the importance of Christ's presence among his followers: "All are called to this union with Christ, who is the light of the world, from whom we go forth, through whom we live, and toward whom our whole life is directed."[14] The way to facilitate the presence of Christ is clear: mutual love and accord, doing the will of God, and loving one another as Christ loved us. His presence among us enables us to fulfill our mission in the church and the world. This reality is consonant with the church as communion, since all are responsible in this communal form of spirituality. Shared experiences of living the word of God and celebrating the eucharist in which burdens are lifted or shared communicate to others the experience of unity and community. This vocation to be in union with Christ and one another is given to all the baptized. It requires the commitment to share responsibility actively, and the maturity to love selflessly.

All parish programs and pastoral initiatives can benefit from regular evaluation. Two critical questions in the evaluation process are: (1) How are we promoting Christ's presence among us when we gather for ministry? (2) Who is responsible for ensuring these conditions are met? Christ's presence among us is the point of departure for all pastoral initiatives, and not the point at which we hope to arrive.

What do you do as a pastoral team to promote this spiritual reality among the various groups engaged in ministry within the parish?

Communion: The Work of God

The modern world has many tensions. In spite of these tensions, one of the signs of the times is a trend toward communion. One example is the ecumenical movement within various churches during the past thirty years. Vatican II spoke of the church as communion and utilized the pre-conciliar work of the Secretariat for Christian Unity to engage in ongoing dialogue with other Christians. This effort toward communion in the world also finds expression in human consciousness, which strives to find a solution for global problems. The cause of communion is promoted by modern means of communication.

The basis for this social order of communion is the Christian perception of communion as the call of Christ for unity with him, and through him with the Father and with each other. Through our baptism, we are called to communion with Christ and one another. Our neighbor provides the way to God for us. We are called to perfect the art of making ourselves one with others: the art of loving (1 Pet 4:8), which involves the fundamental decision to die to self so that Christ may live in us.[15]

Communion requires time to deepen and mature: time spent pondering the word of God, attempting to live out its challenge, and gathering with others to offer the sacrifice of our lives in the eucharist. Our relationship with Christ also requires a reflective spiritual life. Time in prayer enables us to be conscious of the God who dwells within, in whose image we are created, and allows us to recognize our giftedness and respond to his call. Many of the church's clergy suffer from a lack of such prayerful reflection. Many laity, on the other hand, have developed their spirituality as a result of ministerial involvement. Some have developed a great capacity to reflect in the midst of activity. In this respect, clergy can learn much from the laity. In a spirit of humility, all can learn from each other and further develop their spiritual lives.[16]

All the baptized are called to a life of communion, which is nurtured through prayer. Two historical approaches to prayer that enrich our spiritual lives and sustain the call to ministry are (1) the way of images, known as the kataphatic tradition, and (2) the imageless way, known as the apophatic tradition.

The kataphatic approach promotes the use of images and words, particularly the use of the scriptures, to enable the individual to enter more fully into the mystery of faith. The kataphatic tradition enables the individual to find God in all life events. The ultimate meaning of life is discovered in the ministry of Christ, which expresses the ineffable mystery of God. This tradition enables us to discover God in all creation.

The apophatic approach focuses on the inexpressible, unknowable mystery of God. This tradition values the experience of the mystery of the Godhead more than knowledge about the Godhead. The apophatic approach to prayer promotes emptiness, abandoning our own images and thoughts about God.[17] Karl Rahner promoted the image of God as being the incomprehensible mystery.[18] He states, "The communication of mystery can only take place in grace; mystery demands, as the condition of possibility of its being heard, a hearer divinized by grace."[19] Rahner holds that supreme knowledge is knowledge of the supreme mystery as such.[20]

All the baptized are called to utilize various methods of prayer included in these two traditions. The kataphatic tradition of prayer utilizes the scriptures and praying with our senses. The apophatic tradition is evident in centering prayer, which integrates the eastern techniques of utilizing our breathing in prayer and the use of mantras.[21] These various methods of prayer dispose us to receive God's self disclosure, enrich our spiritual lives, and enable us to be more effective in ministry.[22]

Which of the two traditions do you feel most comfortable with? What method of prayer do you promote within the pastoral team and among the various ministries within the parish?

Prayer is the expression of Christian commitment evident in all forms of ministry, and the source of all forms of collaboration.[23] By prayer, God's presence is realized in the midst of his people, and communion grows among the assembly. Listening to God's word provides insight into God's saving work and deepens the bonding within the assembly.[24]

Collaboration is an essential element of spirituality since people have many charisms to share with one another in building up the kingdom of God.[25] Laity and clergy are co-responsible for the mission of the church and complement one another in their ministry. Clergy are perceived to be experts in the spiritual life, yet the laity have an abundance of gifts to use in communion with them. Clergy who are attentive to the laity share their faith experiences with them and accept ministry from them.

I have found the kataphatic approach to be beneficial and stimulating for many people. For example, during a parish assembly gathered to identify pastoral priorities in the church, I invited everyone to take part in an imaginative walk on a beautiful summer day where they saw a sign which said "church." Walking over a hill they saw the reality called "church," where some celebration was in progress. Each felt drawn to go nearer, someone beckoned them to join the assembly, they participated fully in the action, and before they left each received a gift from a member of the "church." Participants shared their different experiences of "church," identified the gifts they received, and explored how they felt as they left the assembly. For some the "church" they described was a current reality, others felt it was an experience of how they wish the "church" to be, still others felt they were participating in a past reality of "church." This experience proved to be equally valuable to ordained and lay ministers, and promoted a lived experience of sharing faith and ecclesial vision.

Sharing spiritual experiences with one another in such a fashion is mutually enriching. Sharing experiences of faith produces trust, understanding, respect, acceptance, and bonding. One phenomenon that manifests an increase in faith-sharing experiences is the reemergence of the tradition of soul-friending.[26] Leonard Doohan in *Grass Roots Pastors* provides a model that promotes the sharing of faith experiences among all engaged in ministry and focuses upon gospel-sharing, shared prayer, shared meditation, group liturgy, communication of life, and group discernment.[27] Sharing of this nature among those engaged in ministry involves vulnerability. When people succeed in sharing experiences of faith, their ability to work collaboratively is enhanced, and communion grows.[28]

I have promoted faith sharing in workshops by asking participants the question: "When have I experienced the risen Lord and whom did I share the experience with?" He was encountered: when the youth raised one thousand dollars in six weeks to go on a weekend retreat, and made a strong commitment to prayer; when my younger brother ministered to our family throughout his terminal illness; in a meditation when the Lord spoke, saying: "Don't you know I only want to love you?"; when I experienced personal trial and weakness, e.g. at the funeral of a close friend I was filled with an awareness of Christ's presence; in the suffering experienced during burnout in ministry, and the new life with Christ I now enjoy. Each time this question was answered, there was always one experience that was shared for the very first time. Sharing our encounters in faith promotes a deeper level of trust and enhances the dignity of all.

What particular method of prayer would you like to explore within the pastoral team? What formation do you need to further promote faith sharing or spiritual mentoring within the parish?

Christ asks that we love one another, which involves service of one's neighbor (Jn 15:13). The cross is the greatest lesson regarding the nature of love. Jesus, crucified and forsaken, makes himself one with his neighbors. He is the model of the person who loves; he is the path and the key to unity with our neighbors. Yet we cannot enter the heart of others and comprehend or share their suffering when our own spirit is preoccupied with a judgment or some worry of our own. Christ calls us to make ourselves one with others, which demands that we be poor in spirit. Only then is communion possible. Making ourselves one implies renunciation (1 Cor 9:2). It is in imitating the love that Christ revealed on the cross that we are able to be one with our neighbor (Jn 17:23). Paul presents the way to promote communion in the model of Christ's obedience to the point of death on the cross (Phil 2:2–5). Gérard Rossé believes that "God assigns man himself the task of going where there is abandonment, division, atheism, and absence of God in order to fill this negativity with his presence."[29]

Imitating the self-sacrificing love of Christ needs to be balanced with time spent in solitude. It is solitude that can fathom the unique dimensions of self, promotes intimacy with oneself, and makes self-donation possible. In solitude we take others with us, our prayer is nourished, and we recognize that communion is indeed the work of God. The experience of solitude develops our consciousness of the indwelling spirit, empowers our growth, promotes self-sacrifice, and fosters collaboration in ministry.[30]

My twelve years' experience in hospital ministry has been very formative. A pattern that has proved invaluable to me is to spend an hour in prayer before entering the hospital, when I enjoy being still, silent and alone with God, and entrust to him the people I will encounter in the hospital. This period of prayer energizes me. Where appropriate I provide pastoral care, counseling, and the sacraments to the staff and sick within the hospital. Each encounter with staff or patient requires a high investment of emotional energy, which means that I often leave the hospital physically, mentally, and spiritually exhausted. I find it necessary to engage in a second period of solitude where I can simply be before God and let God lift me up. At the end of this period of prayer I entrust to God the people I have encountered in the hospital. This solitude and union with God enriches my communion with others, and enables me to be more effective in ministering with others.

The self-sacrificing love of Christ on the cross is the model for all who collaborate in ministry. People involved in team ministry may experience tension and conflict. Examining pastoral needs, discerning the best way to meet them, and evaluating the effectiveness of pastoral initiatives can result in dissension and division. Light is replaced by darkness, peace by anxiety, and joy by sorrow. The members of the team are equally responsible for identifying the causes for the disunity and for ensuring that steps are taken for reinstating a sense of the presence of Christ among the group. When the members of a team love one another as Christ loved us, and are prepared to do the will of God, then the presence of Christ is felt among them. Anxiety is replaced by peace, sorrow by joy, and darkness by light. Responding to pastoral ministry in this way can generate greater trust within the team, which in turn promotes a deeper level of sharing and evokes greater collaboration. Pastoral initiatives can be rendered more effective because Christ is present among the team facilitating and em-powering all in their ministry. An awareness of the presence of Christ among the team can facilitate cooperation, co-responsibility, and communion.

When in your ministry with the pastoral team have you encountered the crucified Christ? What impact did it have on you, and how did you address the situation?

Living the Word

The fathers of the church valued the word of God and encouraged people to live their lives in response to God's word. St. Clement of Alexandria (d. 215) indicated that people are nourished with the seed of life contained in the Bible the same way they nourish themselves with the eucharist.[31] St. Bonaventure (d. 1274) uses the image of a child developing basic skills from others and applies this model to the Christian community growing in faith.[32] The experiences and the insights of individuals are the building blocks of the community's awareness and closeness to Christ.[33]

The proclamation of the word without the testimony of deeds is a scandal to non-Christians today.[34] St. Ambrose (d. 397) urged people to read the scriptures, meditate and pray upon them, so that the Lord is always at work in them.[35] St. Augustine (d. 430) states, "The one who hears the Word of God carelessly will be no less guilty than the one who, out of distraction, lets the

Body of Christ fall to the ground."[36] Vatican II directs: "The treasures of the Bible are to be opened up more lavishly so that a richer share of God's word may be provided for the faithful."[37] It also reinforces the equal importance of the table of the word and the table of the eucharist.[38] Living in response to God's word fosters harmony within the community and makes the eucharistic celebration the summit and source of all forms of collaboration in ministry.

One phrase of scripture that I have lived states: "So I say to you: ask, and it will be given to you; search and you will find; knock, and the door will be opened to you" (Lk 11:9). At the end of the summer I found myself with no money to purchase a ticket to fly home for my vacation, and had prayed expectantly for God's providence to take care of me. It seemed that God was not responding to my constant asking, searching, and knocking. Yet, on the very last evening before I left the parish to go on vacation, I received an unexpected visit from a parishioner who handed me a gift of five hundred dollars to enjoy my vacation. I was excited by this eleventh hour response to my prayer for assistance, and felt that God was saying to me, "See how much I love you." Before departing the next morning I visited a friend who I knew was also struggling financially, and handed over two hundred dollars to assist with his travel. The look of surprise, joy, and wonder on his face was unforgettable.

Paul VI indicates that living the word guarantees happiness, since those who do so are in communication with Christ and possess the kingdom.[39] Living the word of God results in communion with Christ: rejoicing in his dwelling within us and communicating easily with him in times of joy as well as sorrow. This encounter with Christ is not superficial, but results in a profound communion of life (Eph 4:23–24). Living the word involves the reevangelization of a person's way of thinking, willing, and living.

Can you identify one phrase of scripture that has challenged you to radically rethink your ministry? How did you respond to the challenge and what benefits are evident in your ministry within the pastoral team?

Wherever the gospel takes root, the individual is united with Christ and with others. The will of Christ that there be communion among all will be realized where there are Christians who live the word of God (Jn 17:21). St.

Clement of Alexandria (d. 215) indicated that living the word of God generates Christ in persons, in communities, and in churches.[40] In this, all are co-responsible for the building of the kingdom, and the church is experienced as communion. The communion that Christ willed is thus realized, and members of the community become more effective in their call to evangelize society (Jn 17:21).

Many groups and programs currently are operating in parishes, such as Renew, RCIA, Re-membering,[41] Cursillo, etc., yet there is no unifying factor between them. People active within these programs may express a sense of disorientation and fragmentation within the parish community. An essential element seems to be missing from the community. One response to this problem is to unite the various groups around the word of God. The Focolare movement[42] has successfully used a phrase from the Sunday gospel about the word of life to empower the community's response to the challenge of the scriptures.[43] Each parish or home-based faith sharing group takes the same phrase of the gospel, implements it in daily life, and gathers to share the fruits. When existing parish groups take the word of life and share with others how they live it, communion grows among the community. Christ is felt to be present among every group within the parish; his word is alive and active and creates a common focus for all ministry within the community. All pastoral initiatives are enriched by Christ's presence, since communication is improved and responsibility is shared. Living according to God's word helps create unity within the community and generates collaboration in ministry.

My experience of supervising lay ministers engaged in field education has been extensive. One man engaged in a group process of peer evaluation had the most aggressive and cutting remarks to make about others' failures to provide appropriate counseling to enable the client to address pertinent issues. Yet when it came to his turn to be evaluated he rejected the group's continuous claim that he was making blatant basic errors in his own style of counseling. Living the challenge presented in the passage to take the plank out of your own eye first, and then you will see clearly enough to take the splinter that is in your brother's eye (Lk 6:42), enabled him to identify his own deficiencies and begin to address his own issues. I discovered that when each minister seriously attempts to live out this word of God, communication is improved, charity is increased, mutual dignity is promoted, and co-responsibility for the mission of the church is further developed.

Which phrase of the scriptures can you identify as being the most challenging for all engaged in ministry within your parish? How can you encourage every group, organization, and ministry within the parish to live out this phrase of the scriptures and to share their lived experience?

When all the baptized live their lives in response to the word of God the community's experience of the eucharist is enriched. The gathering of the community to celebrate the eucharist is an essential activity of the church. "The liturgy is the summit toward which all the activity of the church is directed; it is also the fount from which all power flows."[44] What are the effects brought about by the celebration of the eucharist?

Realizing Communion in Eucharist

The celebration of the eucharist is central to the life of the early church. In the year 155, Justin describes a liturgical celebration: the assembly listen to the writings of the prophets or memoirs of the apostles; the presider invites all to model their behavior on such experience; prayers are offered, concluding with greeting one another with a kiss; bread and a chalice are offered to the presider, who offers praise, glory, and a lengthy prayer of thanksgiving to God in the name of the assembly, who express their approval by saying "Amen"; deacons distribute the eucharistic bread and also carry it to the absentees.[45]

Justin (d. 165) notes the importance of the real presence during the celebration of the eucharist. The eucharist also reinforces fraternal charity.[46] The Didache states that the eucharistic bread is a symbol of the unity among the brothers and sisters who form the church.[47] St. Irenaeus (d. 200) maintains that God became human in order that humankind may be divinized, and considers the eucharist the cause of the resurrection of the flesh.[48]

Paul VI, in his encyclical *Mysterium Fidei* (1965), retrieves much of the eucharistic tradition and focuses on the eucharist as a memorial, the sacrifice of

Christ and of the church, and a banquet of communion with Christ and with our brothers and sisters. The Constitution on the Liturgy of Vatican II (*Sacrosanctum Concilium*) promotes an active, devout, and educated participation of all in the eucharist. The attention given to the presence of Christ in the assembly has grown in the past ten years, and is seen as related to Christ's presence in the eucharist.[49] All are encouraged to give thanks to God, offer their entire lives to build up the kingdom, and deepen communion with God and with each other.[50]

Our communion with the body and blood of Christ changes us into what we receive.[51] St. Thomas Aquinas (d. 1274) supports this when he states, "The proper effect of the Eucharist is the transformation of the human person into God, one's divinization."[52] John Haughey speaks of the power of the eucharist when he states, "The Eucharist's significative power grows to the degree that the participants find Christ to be real food for their hunger."[53] In being bread for one another, the assembly becomes what it eats in the eucharist. Paul VI holds that the eucharist is instituted to unite us as friends and equals who are called to be of one heart and one soul.[54]

One initiative that has improved the celebration of the eucharist in my present parish has been moving the venue of a weekday eucharistic celebration from the parish church to the local hospital. Previously the assembly were passive and content to be cared for. Now all parishioners come thirty minutes early, prepare the room, gather the sick for the celebration, lead the assembly in praise, and return the sick to the wards afterward. The sick experience a reality of communion with the local community that was previously lacking.

The eucharist incorporates all into Christ, promotes our personal deification, and realizes communion. Yet the Didache states that our disposition during the liturgical celebration is all-important. The basic conditions necessary for the eucharist to produce its full effect are: to believe in the doctrine of Christ, to be baptized, to have faith in what the eucharist is, to live in accordance with the teachings of Christ, to repent and to confess one's sins, to be reconciled to those with whom we are not at peace, to be in unity with the church and with the bishop, and to desire the union with Christ and one's neighbors that the eucharist brings about.[55]

The eucharist invites our participation in the sacred mysteries we celebrate and engages all our faculties: will, intellect, memory, imagination, senses, and body. All are called to recognize the presence of Christ: in the assembly—"Where two or three are gathered together in my name, there I am in the midst of them" (Mt 18:20), in the proclamation of the word through which God directly addresses all, in the eucharistic prayer in which the passion, death, and resurrection of Christ become present, and in the communion service when the consecrated elements of bread and wine are offered to all. Yet the assembly's consciousness of Christ is dependent on the level of preparation for the celebration. The regular practice of kataphatic and apophatic forms of prayer enhances our capacity to identify the presence of Christ in the assembly and respond to the word of God proclaimed in the liturgy. Promoting justice for all, fostering peace in society, and utilizing all our skills to build up the kingdom also prepares us for the celebration of the eucharist.

A friend of mine who attends daily mass was struck by a phrase from Matthew's gospel focusing on the last judgment, "I . . . was in prison and you came to visit me . . ." (Mt 25:36). His cousin's son is in his mid-twenties, has struggled with a depressive illness for years, and earlier this year murdered his mother. The young man's extended family have all deserted him, but David felt that God was asking him to visit his young relative who is now incarcerated for life in a prison for the mentally ill. Although suffering from advanced stages of terminal cancer, David has regularly traveled the four hour journey with his wife to visit his young relative in prison and to offer friendship and compassion to him. David's energy is very limited, yet his only goal each day is to participate in the celebration of the eucharist. He lives out the demands made in Matthew's last judgment each day, and is able to share his many experiences with God during the eucharist, and afterward with those who gather to share their faith.

What does your own remote and proximate preparation for the celebration of the eucharist consist of? What resources could be made available in your parish to improve the assembly's preparation for the eucharistic celebration?

Karl Rahner held that the eucharist celebrates the mystery of the absolute nearness of God. Celebrating the eucharist empowers all in the call to ministry. The communion with Christ and with the assembly celebrated in the eucharist makes all more conscious of the supreme presence, and commissions all to be agents of evangelization in the world.[56]

All are incorporated into Christ by baptism and become members of the people of God as priests, prophets, and kings. The call to ministry flowing from baptism into the royal priesthood consists in bringing the spiritual sacrifices of one's whole life to witness to Christ over all the earth (1 Pet 2:4–10). All ministry is enhanced by the individual's union with Christ. Every Christian has the same spiritual aids common to all, among which the active participation in the eucharist "is especially to be recommended."[57]

What is particular to the universal priesthood is their relation with Christ; their growth in holiness is achieved in their activity in the world. This is their special way to greater holiness. Thus believers are sanctified in the course of their life and participation in society. For the Christian, the world cannot be construed as hostile or obstructive to the spirit; rather the Christian, by virtue of his or her vocation, brings to the world a new richness in the stamp of Christ.

The sources of spiritual nourishment available to all include: meditating on the word of God through which one comes to personal knowledge of Christ (Phil 3:8), responding in prayer to the word of God (D.V. 25), and celebrating the eucharist (1 Cor 10:14–18). All are called to a holistic form of spirituality that embraces the totality of existence, including all relationships, every occupation, and the relationship of all with the environment. God's Spirit is at work in all aspects of our lives. Utilizing all our resources in a holistic form of spirituality deepens communion and promotes the collaboration of all in building up the kingdom.[58]

What funding, materials, and workshops are available to the pastoral team and other leaders of ministries within the parish for promoting personal spiritual development?

All members of the church share in the ministry of spreading the gospel of Christ, thereby mediating his grace. The special function of the ministerial priesthood in the service of word and sacraments does not exclude the universal priesthood from exercising a very important role in this ministry, since the service of the pastors and the ministry of the laity mutually complement one another. The world receives the proclamation of Christ through the life of

Christians nourished on the word and the eucharist. The Christian community is united with Christ in the eucharist and is called to do what Christ has done: give its life for the world.

The celebration of the eucharist reveals Christ's presence in his sacramental body and manifests the depth of communion that exists among the people of God.[59] The entire assembly utilize their gifts to build up the kingdom. The skills of all the assembly are exercised during the celebration of the eucharist and include hospitality, fellowship, proclamation, intercession, praising, thanksgiving, and nurturing. The active participation of all the assembly during the celebration of the eucharist builds communion and expresses the collaborative nature of ministry. The eucharist is thus the fountain from which all ministry flows and the living spring that sustains all engaged in ministry.

Summary

All the baptized are called to recognize their own dignity and the dignity of others, since all are created in the image and likeness of God and as the people of God participate in the ministry of the church as leaven in the world. They are sanctified by the gospel of Christ through their activity in society. Christ gathers us and calls us to the service of building up the kingdom and instills in his church the sense of collegiality and communion. It is Christ's presence within the individual and among the community that facilitates the holiness of those engaged in pastoral ministry.

The spiritual foundation of the community rests on the recognition of Christ's presence in the individual and in the community. This presence empowers all to share responsibility for the mission of the church, fulfills their call as disciples of Christ, and generates communion within the church. Living out the word of God unites every member of the community with Christ, who generates mutual respect and facilitates co-responsibility in ministry.

Collaboration in ministry is a reality in which power and responsibility are shared by the people of God who recognize the spiritual leadership of the pastor. Collaboration flows from mutual respect and is a sign of equality in faith. It requires an attentiveness to the Spirit in others and demands an ongoing form of discernment. The presence of Christ empowers cooperation, coresponsibility, and communion in the ecclesial community.

The eucharist celebrates the equal dignity of all as members of the people of God, promotes reconciliation among all, assists all in the process of divinization, sustains all in the call to ministry, and promotes the collaboration of all in building up the kingdom.

All the baptized are called to collaborate in service of the church, share responsibility for the mission of the church, and promote communion within the church and society. A spiritual foundation for collaborative ministry enables these commitments to be fulfilled. Such a spiritual foundation incorporates the following components: it is holistic in the integration of prayer, ministry, and liturgical celebration with mission, it promotes the reality of the church as communion, it enables all to collaborate more effectively in ministry, and it utilizes the particular skills of all in building up the kingdom.[60]

The style of leadership adopted within a parish is significant: it promotes cooperation, develops collaborative styles of management, and deepens communion within the parish. The relational dynamics that facilitate collaborative ministry and develop communion need to be explored. What are the interpersonal skills and leadership styles that promote collaboration in ministry and develop communion within the local church? Are particular skills necessary for collaborative ministry? How can these skills be learned? What leadership style best promotes co-responsibility in ministry, utilizes the gifts of all, and deepens communion?

Chapter III responds to these questions and outlines the interpersonal skills and leadership styles that promote communion and develop collaborative ministry within the parish.

Reflection

1. A phrase of scripture that I have lived, made incarnate in my life, and is significant for me is . . .

2. A way of praying that I find most useful is . . .

3. A method of faith-sharing that appeals to me is . . .

4. A liturgical celebration that most appeals to me is . . .

Suggested Reading

1. Wilkie Au, *By Way of the Heart: Toward a Holistic Christian Spirituality.*
    Mahwah: Paulist Press, 1989.

2. John Dalrymple, *Letting Go in Love: Reflections on Spiritual Formation.*
    Wilmington: Michael Glazier, 1988.

3. Chiara Lubich, *From Scripture to Life.* New York: New City Press, 1991.

CHAPTER III

The Leadership Styles That Facilitate Collaborative Ministry

Four pastors who had promoted collaborative models of ministry were contacted to see if they were interested in participating in a workshop aimed at developing collaborative ministry within the pastoral team. All four stated that, since the focus of the workshop concerned the pastoral team, the facilitator should provide a presentation of the nature, goals, and process utilized in the workshop at the subsequent pastoral team meeting. In each case the pastor did not wish to be given any prior information that could make him biased for or against implementing the workshop. The facilitator gave a brief presentation to each pastoral team, answered questions, and gave each team two weeks in which to decide whether or not they wished to establish a contract. All four pastoral teams reached a consensus which led to the implementation of the workshop in each parish.

In earlier times most pastors would have invited the facilitator to send him the materials first so that he could judge whether the pastoral team should be given information regarding the workshop, thus controlling the kind of development in the pastoral team. Pastors, who together with their pastoral team experience academic, spiritual, and interpersonal formation, are intent on implementing the teachings of Vatican II and look beyond traditional forms of ministry. The commitment of the pastoral team to engage in parish pastoral development promotes closer union with Christ, utilizes the resources of the faith community, and enhances belief in Christ in the wider community. The key focus in this process is communion and collaboration.

Since Vatican II, many manifestations of communion and collaboration have sprung up in parish communities. Ministries that use the time and talent of individuals for the service of the community in liturgy and music, education and sacraments, leadership and pastoral activity have grown. Within parishes, people gather in groups of one kind or another to develop faith along particular lines of interest. However, this transition from the traditional stance of a church of passive recipients to a church responsible for the formation and growth of the people of God takes place in a haphazard way. The success of particular initiatives depends on the charisms of individuals and their ability to attract the attention of the community at large for a particular venture.

This chapter examines the processes involved in promoting communion and collaboration within the parish framework. Of particular interest are the features of this process that form the basis for cooperation, communion, and collaboration in today's parish. These features are: (1) the organizational models that promote collaboration in ministry, (2) the leadership styles necessary for further developing collaborative ministry, (3) the supervision of ministry within the pastoral team, and (4) the training that fosters collaborative ministry.

The Organization of Ministry

Within the past thirty years, various groups have been formed to minister within parishes. These groups are characterized by (1) diversity of background, expertise and lifestyle, (2) division of labor, and (3) cooperation in a common task. Talents are varied and specialization in ministry is coordinated through planning sessions. Different lifestyles are evident, be they clerical or lay, celibate or married, communal or solitary. A principle of group ministry is the recognition of the diversity of charisms within the community and facilitating their expression. In this process, collaboration between clergy and laity is essential for the church's mission.[1]

The vision that the local church has of the universal church is evident in the way it organizes its communal life. Different styles of parish organization promote principles of collegiality and shared responsibility and express the baptismal rights of the people of God in different ways.

The Classic Style   One of the features of this model assumes that the primary purpose of the parish is to transmit its heritage. Attention is paid to maintaining the status quo and an orderly growth in faith based on tried and tested methods. The faithful experience a strong sense of security, nostalgia, and a sense of being rooted. Many people experienced the church in this way: they, their children, and grandchildren went through the system of parochial schools, received the sacraments at specified stages in their personal development, participated in the life of the community in Sunday and daily mass, and attended the occasional social function. Today such people are shaken by the "cafeteria approach" to the church, whereby individuals pick and choose aspects of church teaching, practice, and insights that appeal to their individualism and leave the rest. The traditional style of parish meets the needs of many parishioners, but is not open to new sources of vitality and growth. Authority and power are primarily in the hands of the clergy, with little attempt to empower laity in ministry.[2]

In this model, each person fits into a ready-made structure that is hierarchical, highly structural, and heavily dependent on the delegation of authority. The strength of this style of parish is that everyone knows where he or she stands. The chain of command is clear and allows innovation while protecting the structure of the system. This same structure limits creative and spontaneous initiatives, vitality, and interdependence, since all new ideas must be incorporated into an existing framework, which easily creates dependency.[3]

The Charismatic or Intuitive Style   This style depends on the charisma of the pastor and the dynamism and validity of his vision. This style of leadership rejects the status quo and is open to initiative and spontaneity. Its strength is its vitality and flexibility, which appeals to the more liberated Catholic. The weakness is that this style revolves around the charismatic personality of the pastor, which often leads to the disintegration of all programs when he is replaced. Another difficulty is the pastor's "in group" whose members are frequently too dependent on him.[4]

The Human Relations Style   This style develops good team spirit and close relations among the staff. It promotes group development and generates a high degree of commitment and personal satisfaction. Here the dignity of each team member is respected and there is a strong sense of support. The danger is that the team may become a comfortable clique in which disturbing issues are not addressed. Interests are promoted in the community without reference to their relative value, and the community becomes the church of the like-minded, concerned with a narrow band of particular issues. Suppression of such issues can lead to explosive outbursts in the team.[5]

The Systematic Style   This approach to pastoral ministry helps people identify their gifts and empowers people to use them. In this type of parish, the emphasis is on shared authority and mutual ministry. There is a real respect for each person's gifts, a common objective, and goals toward which all strive. Each member is conscious of his or her own charisms, yet mindful of the mission of the community. This style breaks the traditional mold in which the priest is seen as having all the charisms and all the power. This style can cause divisions between those who want the traditional roles to remain intact and those who are active in lay ministry.[6]

     The systematic style of parish is the one that most reflects the ecclesiology of communion, in which each member of the people of God is respected and valued. The principles that guide the pastor are (1) the ability to encourage others to identify and carry out their mission, (2) the conviction that interdependency is preferable to dependency, and (3) an endeavor that equips, supports, confirms, and serves the ministry of all the baptized.[7] This style of leadership is a collaborative one in which dreams, vision, hopes, and experiences are shared.

Developing Collaboration in Ministry

The team model of ministry facilitates sharing and mutual commitment in mission and ministry. This style of collegiate leadership calls everyone to a different level of maturity and communion. Collaboration in ministry demands a greater depth of self-awareness, in that it calls for a level of cooperation that is less dependent, more self-revealing and demands a commitment to emotional honesty and the willingness to deal with conflict in a mature way. A collaborative vision of ministry perceives authority as the creative capacity to call forth the vision and gifts of others. In this context authority invites rather than controls, nurtures rather than constricts.[8]

My most powerful experience of calling forth the gifts of others took place during my year spent in a formation community in Frascati, Italy. My sharing group consisted of six people from Argentina, Italy, Portugal, Scotland, Spain, and Switzerland. After six months engaged in sharing our material and spiritual goods, we took part in an exercise of mutual affirmation. Each of the group received one hour of affirmation: the first thirty minutes consisted of identifying the particular gifts and strengths of the individual; the second thirty minutes were spent identifying the particular weaknesses of every member of the group. Our common experience during the time spent in "affirmation" was that it provided a staggering degree of insight, compassion, encouragement, and appreciation. Yet the "critique and evaluation" we all received during the second thirty minutes was also extremely accurate, penetrating, truthful, challenging, and uplifting. The most powerful experience during the entire six hours of the exercise was the depth of mutual charity.

What has been your most nourishing experience in your formation for ministry? How have you developed your ability to nurture and call forth the gifts in others?

The parish teams[9] that invest time in studying together, sharing prayer, and participating in team-building promote a greater depth of self-awareness, honesty, and maturity. These activities enable team members to affirm and challenge each other in ways that are life-giving. Celebrating liturgy together and spending time on retreat also promote the development of collaboration in ministry.[10]

Parishes that have clear job descriptions promote role clarification within the parish team and enable the pastoral team to be accepted by the community. Laity require the same degree of support which is offered to clergy for ongoing formation to enable all ministers to further develop particular charisms. Yet tension, criticism, and negativity often limit effective motivation of others. Progress and success are often curtailed by the same negative influences. Many full-time lay ministers have little long-term security since contracts are frequently renewed on a yearly basis. These problems need to be addressed since they can contribute to depression and burnout and result in people leaving the ministry.[11]

The leadership style that a pastoral team utilizes can either promote or hinder the development of communion which manifests itself in various forms of collaborative ministry. What leadership styles actively promote mutual respect among all, the sharing of responsibility, and consensus decision-making?

The Semi-Mutual Style of Leadership

The semi-mutual style emerged in the early 1970s and appears to be the favorite style of pastoral leadership in some Christian churches. It is similar to the company executive relating to the board of directors or trustees. The Catholic Church in America has many parish pastoral teams whose practice is semi-mutual, but their experience in ministry usually is not genuinely collaborative. Although there is a clear division of labor and some joint accountability, autonomy is stressed at the expense of collaboration.

The semi-mutual style of leadership stresses joint responsibility for the performance of the agreed tasks. A team operating according to this model gets together periodically to set a basic plan for their work, but in the daily execution of pastoral tasks, the staff members operate in parallel fashion. Interaction clarifies goals and objectives. The best this style can offer is weekly staff meetings at which the business of the week is reviewed and assigned. The team has an understanding of the work required. Interaction throughout the week is more informal and social rather than professional.[12]

Typical Relationships in the Semi-Mutual Style

Individual members are respected and have a sense of responsibility in the planning process. Authority is shared in the group because there is a collective responsibility for planning and setting goals. When the team gathers to build a consensus around its goals, it makes collaborative decisions. Such planning can be very stressful.[13]

Strengths   The semi-mutual style of leadership offers a sense of balance when attempting to achieve goals and objectives. There is a sense of openness to planning and a strong focus on task. Such interaction among leaders creates communion within the team which makes this style appealing in many parish settings. This style offers substantial coordination among leaders for a minimal investment of time.[14]

Weaknessess   This style fails to integrate planning and performance. The planning is done by the leadership group, but the benefits end there. The plan is not carried out as a team, since its ministry is exercised in isolation, which in turn causes difficulties. Individual ministers end up implementing a plan that has emerged from the group's agenda, not from their own, and may not feel able to implement the delegated plan. Some tasks are assigned to individuals who do not have the necessary competence to implement them, since the team may be unaware who has the necessary skills to produce clear results. Planning suffers due to the fact that the integrated vision of the team is not applied to the implementation. In this system limited knowledge of one's peers restricts effective peer review, which is required to complete the task. The high stress associated with this style can spill over into day-to-day performance of the team, diminishing cooperation and rendering ministry ineffective. This style of leadership needs other means to strengthen the communion among team members, such as spiritual, social, and off-the-job interaction.[15]

The pastor of one pastoral team I worked with described his style of leadership as being more "comprehensive" than the semi-mutual style. His perception was that authority is shared within the group, and that consensus is the norm of all pastoral team decisions. Yet several members of the pastoral team stated clearly: "Our pastor is very gifted, but he does not listen—he has his own agenda, and all pastoral development must fit into the priorities of his vision."

This lack of mutual awareness between the pastor and the members of the pastoral team is common. Many pastors use the language of shared responsibility, yet fail to exercise it.

What leadership style have you experienced in your ministry that has been life-giving? What qualities are necessary for effective leadership in ministry today?

The Mutual Style of Leadership

The mutual style of pastoral leadership emerged in the late 1970s and currently operates in few parish pastoral teams. One example is found in the members of a retreat team who regularly work together and who operate as interchangeable parts in the system, since their work together enables them to learn each other's skills. Individual personality and style are highly valued, yet each member's performance retains a distinctive identity. The mutual style puts strong emphasis on the sharing of authority, accountability, and labor. Authority is corporate, with every team member sharing in decision-making as well as in policy-making. The team members are mutually accountable for providing appropriate feedback.[16]

In the mutual style, leadership is shared since the ideal is that tasks be performed collaboratively whenever possible. There is a new stress on the internal integration of leaders: (1) they need to be well balanced and emotionally and developmentally stable; (2) the ongoing integration of the members of the team depends on the mutual support they receive from their integration with each other; (3) interaction implies that the leadership integrates various leadership tasks so that they form a coherent and systematic unit.[17]

In this mutual style, responsibility is shared not only in deciding goals and objectives, but also in joint responsibility for their performance. Unlike the semi-mutual style, the leaders have on-the-job interaction, which facilitates co-responsibility and communion. Those who work according to this style experience profound equality and interchangeability of role. Relationships among team members reveal a high level of interdependence, since all rely on each other. Authority in this mutual style also is shared where co-responsibility is a reality within the team. Team members rely on each other's personal integrity to support their own professional effectiveness. Deep-rooted trust in the abilities and competence of other people facilitates communion within the team, where control over the way tasks are accomplished is surrendered.[18]

Strengths   The mutual style of leadership is attractive to many groups, because it creates communion, but it does not work effectively in every ministerial setting. The mutual style often looks better on paper than it does in reality. Yet it does have strengths: the ongoing interaction between leaders and their presence to one another fosters high-quality relationships that are mutually supportive. Isolation is overcome and integration wins against fragmentation. When it operates effectively, the mutual style creates communion where the wide range of resources, skills, and charisms of the team interlock in a way that reflects the wholeness of church and ministry. All learn through such interaction and are able to observe each other's performance, affirm, and offer valuable feedback. The deep level of sharing among equals provides opportunities for growth and learning. It offers freedom on many levels: to be imperfect, to be vulnerable, to rely on others in one's ministry, to struggle, to fail, and to grow. This freedom attracts many to adopt this style of leadership and is its most profound asset.[19]

Weaknesses   Those in the mutual style are never alone, which imposes the burden of group maintenance. This involves commitment: (1) to facilitating group interaction while responding to the dynamics of the group, (2) to providing time for planning, supervision, evaluation, feedback, prayer, and socializing, and (3) to balancing the time and energy invested in pastoral tasks against the time invested in the group's own maintenance. Many involved in ministry find these types of commitments unrealistic. The mutual style of leadership demands investment in the ministry of others and commitment to a labor-intensive use of personnel resources that most parishes find unacceptable.[20]

The surrender of personal autonomy and independence to the authority of the group can be oppressive. All of one's ministry is watched by others and subject to group evaluation. The process of decision-making is cumbersome, since it extends to routine, urgent, and trivial issues. A pre-condition for this style is a high investment in decision-by-consensus on the part of its members. This style attracts people who are looking for community and friendship as well as professional support, but is unable to fulfill these needs.[21]

Each pastoral team I worked with raised similar questions: "Is there a natural progression from the classic style, to the semi-mutual style, then onto the mutual-style of leadership? Should we be aiming to work more toward the mutual-style of leadership?" The mutual-style has more universal appeal to pastoral teams, yet is less well suited to being the operative model of leadership utilized in most parish ministries. The high investment of time, energy, and resources required to train everyone in a multiplicity of ministries, combined with the large investment of time required for group formation, development, and evaluation, makes this an inappropriate model of leadership.

What is the most dominant style of leadership exercised in your pastoral team? Does the leadership style promote the dignity of all and further the experience of communion among all?

Choosing the right model of leadership generates cooperation, co-responsibility, and communion within team ministry. Those involved in ministry can select ingredients from the various styles that fulfill their pastoral needs while facilitating collaboration in ministry.

In the classic style, the individual is accountable for two things: (1) the demonstration of obedience to authority by carrying out one's assignments, and (2) the support of the agenda of those in authority. After Vatican II, local clergy became accountable for introducing a series of pastoral reforms in their parishes, where they either defend the status quo or are the agents of change. In the traditional style, accountability to immediate superiors is the norm and consists in reporting progress on assigned tasks.[22]

In the semi-mutual style of leadership, the burden of accountability for the day-to-day tasks rests on the individual. Joint planning makes the individual periodically accountable to the other leaders. Planning involves reviewing the implementation of previous plans and evaluating their success, with the focus more on general priorities than on specific tasks. Knowing that accountability is required encourages conscientiousness in addressing various tasks.[23]

In the mutual style of leadership the work and accountability for it is shared in a reciprocal way, rather than one-way. The tasks are worked out collaboratively, and team members are accountable to themselves and colleagues. Since it is reciprocal, this style leads to individual accountability within the team.[24]

Supervision Within the Pastoral Team

A member of a parish pastoral team put this question to the associate pastor "Whom are you accountable to, and who supervises your ministry?" The young priest replied with a smile, "I am only held accountable by my bishop, but he would only intervene if I made a major mess of things."

All members of parish pastoral teams regularly have to give an account of their various programs and ministries to the pastor. Most professional lay ministers experience an annual evaluation of their ministry which leads to their contract being terminated or renewed. The associate pastor is often the least experienced member of the pastoral team, has less specialized competence, and has no particular program to resource or develop. It is understandable that many professional lay ministers strongly resent the fact that unlike them the associate pastor's ministry is not supervised, nor does he render an account of his stewardship. Associate pastors often perceive any form of pastoral supervision in a negative light, and fail to comprehend that pastoral supervision promotes personal formation, professional development, and collaboration in ministry. Supervision enables ministers to reflect on their experience and learn from that reflection by adequately preparing for future tasks. All engaged in formation for ministry can benefit from professional supervision and evaluation. Yet this presents a problem for several styles of pastoral leadership.

The classic style is not geared for support and supervision: the minister is assigned a task, performs it, and then reports back that it is accomplished. Any kind of supervision that is given often is given informally or socially and focuses solely on the pastor. The frequency and quality of support in this style depends largely on the personality of the one in ultimate authority.[25]

The support and supervision in the semi-mutual style addresses pastoral priorities, not day-to-day tasks. Support is offered while plans are made but not in their implementation. In the mutual style, the support and supervision must be built in and needs to be ongoing and consistent, since the ministers are involved at every level of planning and implementation. The support and supervision also must be available on a formal and informal basis and needs to address both planning and actual performance.[26]

The first two styles of leadership fail to make adequate provision for support and supervision. The trade-off in the mutual style is different: support and supervision are an integral part of this system, which calls for a high investment of time and energy to make it work. In the mutual style, mutual support and supervision cannot be avoided.[27] All engaged in ministry can benefit from some form of supervision, either in a group process or one-on-one, where all are accountable for the way gifts are utilized to build up the kingdom and provided with the resources necessary for personal development. When an individual's ministry requires or benefits from support and supervision, this needs to be integrated within the operative style.

During an interview I had with an archbishop the question arose: "How do you help ministers receive appropriate support and supervision in ministry, particularly when they are showing signs of burnout?" I asked the bishop: "What was your experience of ongoing evaluation or supervision in ministry when you were a priest in the diocese, and has this changed since you became archbishop seven years ago?" He replied: "I have no experience of ongoing evaluation or supervised ministry!" I replied: "What makes you think that the clergy will listen to you now, when you encourage them to engage in something that is outside your experience?" It's no surprise that the clergy struggle with "receiving support" when most were trained to be autonomous and self-sufficient, and perceive any form of evaluation in a negative light. The challenge, I told the archbishop, was for him to model a leadership style where he is involved in the process of "supervised ministry." Then he will know what it feels like, will benefit from the ongoing evaluation, and can share his lived experience with those ministers who are showing signs of stress in their ministry.

What has been your best experience of supervision in ministry? What models of supervised ministry would you like to explore within your pastoral team?

Training for Collaborative Ministry

Training includes the acquisition of knowledge, positive attitudes, mastery of particular skills, and competence in the role of pastoral leadership. Training fosters communion and collaboration within the team. The leadership style adopted in team ministry affects the whole training process.

The classic style requires knowledge and attitudes that are theological, theoretical, and hierarchical. The church as institution is essential in the vision of this style and produces individuals who are competent and subordinate. The necessary skills focus on ministerial performance: presiding, preaching, reconciling, counseling, and catechizing. Adopting appropriate etiquette is necessary when dealing with superiors or subordinates.[28]

The semi-mutual style of leadership stresses the importance of planning as well as theological instruction and is more oriented to renewal and is more creative and imaginative than the classic style. Training for this style instills a sense of vision and develops the ability to set goals and objectives, and implement, coordinate, and evaluate plans and programs. The semi-mutual style also builds self-confidence and a sense of autonomy and responsibility in implementing goals. Training involves cooperation, co-responsibility, and evaluation of each stage of a plan by the team. The persons best suited to this style are able to relate well with others and facilitate communion without being subordinate in the exercise of their particular ministry.[29]

Training for the mutual style builds on an attitude that values collaboration. Collaboration is seen in this mutual style of ministry as being urgent, practical, and of great personal importance. Training for this type of ministry requires (1) a sophisticated understanding of personal development, (2) a firm grasp of interpersonal dynamics, such as trust, cooperation, and justice, (3) the ability to reflect theologically, and (4) the ability to discern the different roles of colleagues.[30]

The training requirements for the various styles of leadership are cumulative: starting from the classic style leading to the mutual style, training becomes more complex. Training for ministry prepares people better for one particular style than for another. But any real match between training and style often is coincidental. Training enhances the person's effectiveness and facilitates collaboration in ministry.[31] Filling vacancies in the parish pastoral team is made easier by matching the team's style and the candidates' training. Attending to this link facilitates co-responsibility, communion, and collaboration in ministry.[32]

The Exercise of Power   The members of the parish pastoral team are leaders in their own sphere of activity. Effective pastoral planning and care depends on the leadership style of the team. There are many styles of leadership, but no single style addresses every situation, and not all leaders have the same gifts. Sharing leadership within the parish team results in collaboration within the group, where successful initiatives are implemented in the complex field of pastoral action.[33]

Consultation identifies needs and sets goals and objectives. Where matters of faith and pastoral ministry are at stake, the aim is service of others, not the exercise of decisive power.[34] There is a joint responsibility to do what is best for the church and its mission. The way responsibility is shared within the team is crucial. The process that leads to decisions determines the quality of the final decision, which grows in proportion to the applied gifts of the people involved in the decision. Consultation involves agreement to use the gifts of all toward a decision which serves others.[35]

I was contracted to do a two hour workshop with a pastoral council focusing on "the church's vision of a parish pastoral council." The council had representatives from every ministry within the parish and had been in existence for one year. During the session I led the group in prayer and faith-sharing, gave a presentation on the role and vision of the church regarding parish pastoral councils, and enabled the council to share their vision of what the pastoral council is called to be. At the end of the session the consensus was that the council would hold an extraordinary meeting to process the meeting and develop a mission statement for the council. The only dissenting voice was that of the coordinator of the council who stated, "As I see it we have just decided to end the pastoral council," to which the pastor replied, "as we had previously experienced it!"

The council members were elated by the consultative process utilized in the workshop whereby power was shared and told me, "You should have been here a year ago when we were just starting!"

What has been your best experience of working with a consultant? What do you need to develop your skills as a consultant in your particular ministry?

Communication and Communion   Communication within the parish pastoral team is not an end in itself. Communication, fostered through sharing feelings about common experiences and values, involves trust as well as risk. The team experience provides the opportunity for every member to enrich relationships, contributes to the call to ministry, and helps individuals grow in following Christ.[36]

Confidentiality is important for the effective ministry of the parish pastoral team and must be observed by all. The leader needs to emphasize the importance of confidentiality at various stages of the group's development. When confidentiality has been breached the sense of communion within the group diminishes. Each member of the group is co-responsible for addressing this problem. When members speak about what they learned in group sessions, confidentiality is respected, but when they talk about how they acquired insights or what they did in the group, confidentiality is likely to be breached.[37]

Conflict and Confrontation   Conflicts within a group are inevitable. Not facing up to conflict leads to defensive behavior, hostility, indirectness, and a lack of trust. When handled successfully, conflict increases the level of trust within the group and creates a deeper sense of communion.[38] Cohesion and positive feelings about the group increase when negative feelings are addressed. The mature group learns to sustain an honest level of challenge, the best way of resolving conflict in a group. Decisions arrived at, using the strategy of problem-solving, in which consensus decision-making is normative, produce a final solution that is acceptable to all.[39] Qualities that manifest themselves in healthy conflict management are: (1) a good relationship between the parties allows them to accept conflict as part of growth; (2) each member of the group is involved in resolving the crises; (3) those in conflict must deal with facts and not motives; (4) the issue is dealt with briefly, is resolved, and both sides accept the consequences of conflict without bearing grudges.[40]

Confrontation often is seen in a negative light.[41] Yet leaders need to confront each group member, inviting them to explore some aspect of their interpersonal style of their life to determine whether they wish to change. The quality of the confrontations within a group is an indication of the effectiveness of the group. The greater the cohesion and communion within the group, the more challenging the confrontation.[42]

One of the most heated discussions I experienced during my ministry with pastoral teams was the exchange between two members during a session on discernment. One minister stated, "I fundamentally disagree with the ecclesial vision contained in the background reading we were asked to prepare for this meeting. I have more red ink in the preface than the author has black ink!" The other team member said, "I found the material exciting, stimulating, and just the kind of vision we need for ministry in our parish." I suggested that it was vital that these essential differences in vision of church be explored if the pastoral team were to develop collaborative forms of ministry. But one of the ministers walked out of the meeting and chose not to participate in the subsequent five sessions of the workshop.

The communication during the subsequent five sessions of the workshop were less heated and the conflict was more masked. But the minister who opted out had an invaluable contribution to make to the pastoral team. Because of his directness and honesty, issues that created conflict were identified and addressed. The confrontation he invoked increased the level of honest communication within the rest of the team.

When have you experienced conflict and confrontation within the pastoral team? In what ways has it challenged you to development your communication skills?

Feedback and Evaluation   Feedback highlights blind spots, aids the assessment of performance, and encourages work on weaknesses within the program.[43] Feedback can pinpoint where collaboration is superficial and communion is shallow. In the classic style, the only feedback that carries any weight comes from the immediate superior. Feedback from the team is superficial, since it is based on the observation of infrequent team meetings. Evaluations often are inaccurate and not constructive, since they are based on chance encounters between the person in authority and the person on the job. Evaluation tends to be judgmental, reflecting one person's perspective, and results in team members viewing it in a negative light.[44]

The semi-mutual style provides feedback and evaluation that is random and inconsistent. Feedback is easy when the team is at the planning stage, but nearly impossible when people are left to perform their tasks in isolation. Since individuals interact mainly at the planning stage and not during implementation, they lack an adequate basis for evaluating one another's work. Individuals receive positive feedback and evaluation regarding their effectiveness during the implementation.[45]

Feedback and evaluation, like support and supervision, are integral and essential to the mutual style. A portion of the time is given over to feedback and evaluation. Each group member shares responsibility for the growth and development of the whole team. In addition to fulfilling the individual's tasks at the planning stage, responsibility is assumed for on-the-job growth and development of other team members. The time spent providing support and affirmation to other group members needs to be balanced against the time engaged in ministering to others outside the group. Such feedback and evaluation increase cooperation, co-responsibility, and communion within team ministry.[46] Since mutual style involves collaboration, colleagues have abundant data against which the achievement of goals can be assessed. When feedback and evaluation are given, this increases trust, promotes better performance, and facilitates collaboration, which makes the mutual style attractive and enjoyable.[47]

One pastoral team I worked with scheduled an hour of feedback and evaluation for all members of the staff each month. The pastor was competent, skilled in group process and trained in the development of lay ministry. He met individually with each member of the staff for an hour each month to review programs, provide supervision in ministry, and explore opportunities for development. I asked the pastor, "Whom do you go to for supervision of your ministry?" He replied, "I don't go regularly to anyone." I challenged the pastoral team to explore the process of "group supervision of ministry" which would include the pastor in the group's evaluation of ministry.

All who utilize their skills in supervision in ministry, counseling, and pastoral evaluation should themselves experience ongoing supervision in ministry, counseling, and evaluation.

What is your experience of supervised ministry? What resources are available to the pastoral team to engage in ongoing pastoral formation and professional development?

Summary

The leadership style chosen by parish pastoral teams should promote communion and collaboration within the parish community. The leadership style of each parish is manifested through the pastor's vision of the church, combined with the leadership and counseling skills of the pastoral team. Members of parish pastoral teams have the opportunity to enrich relationships, develop their gifts of service to the community, and assist the growth of others in their following of Christ. Consultation within the parish pastoral team is essential for the identification of needs and the setting of goals, and the quality of the consultation grows in proportion to the applied gifts of the people involved in the consultation. Communication within the pastoral team fosters communion. Conflict is inevitable in the group process, but when handled successfully it leads to an increased level of trust and communion within the parish pastoral team. The greater the co-responsibility and cohesion, the more challenging the confrontation.

The classic style of pastoral leadership is hierarchical, highly relational, and heavily dependent on the delegation of authority. Everyone knows where he or she stands, and the chain of command is clear and allows for innovation while protecting the structure of the system. The same structure limits vitality and interdependence, since all new ideas must be incorporated into an existing framework. This style limits creative and spontaneous initiatives, creates too much dependency on the leader, and stifles co-responsibility.

The semi-mutual style of pastoral leadership offers a sense of balance in which the goals of cooperation and co-responsibility are realized. There is a strong sense of openness to planning, with the focus on the task. It offers substantial coordination among leaders and increases collaboration in ministry for a minimal investment of time. Interaction among leaders makes this style appealing to many parish pastoral teams, yet it fails to integrate planning with performance, while requiring spiritual, social, and on-the-job interaction to strengthen the bond of communion among team members.

The mutual style of pastoral leadership promotes the sharing of authority, accountability, and labor. Leadership is shared and tasks are performed in collaboration. The leaders have on-the-job interaction, which facilitates inter-dependency within the team. This style is attractive, since it creates communion, provides a deep level of sharing, and facilitates learning. This leadership style requires a commitment to minister together, which is labor-intensive in personnel resources and requires decision by consensus.

The parish pastoral team should choose the operative style of leadership that facilitates its mission and ministry. Co-responsibility, communion, and collaboration are facilitated within the parish pastoral team by accountability, support, supervision, feedback, evaluation, and training.

The interpersonal skills and leadership styles that promote collaborative ministry incorporate the ecclesiological and spiritual foundation in a concrete form. The ecclesiological foundation articulates that we are called to be church, the spiritual foundation articulates how we can become that reality, and the chosen leadership style determines who is involved in the process.

Each parish expresses the universal mission of the church within its locality. What process enables a parish to articulate its mission within the diocese? Can different perceptions of the ecclesiological, spiritual, and interpersonal dimensions of collaboration be integrated into a mission statement? Why is it necessary to develop a parish pastoral plan of action? How does developing a mission statement and implementing a pastoral plan of action deepen communion within the parish? A discernment process is needed to articulate a parish mission statement that respects pluralism and diversity in the parish. How does the development of a parish mission statement and the implementation of a pastoral plan of action promote communion?

Chapter IV responds to these questions by proposing a way of integrating theory, reflection, and pastoral development. The Vatican II documents stimulate reflection wherein parish pastoral development is evaluated.

Reflection

1. One insight I gained from reflecting on various styles of leadership utilized in pastoral teams is . . .

2. One issue that creates conflict within our pastoral team and needs to be addressed is . . .

3. Communication, trust and accountability can be promoted in our pastoral team if we were willing to . . .

Suggested Reading

1. Robert G. Duch, *Successful Parish Leadership: Nurturing the Animated Parish.* Kansas City: Sheed and Ward, 1990.

2. Mary B. McKinney, *Sharing Wisdom: A Process for Group Decision Making.* Allen: Tabor Publishing Co., 1989.

3. Bernard F. Swain, *Liberating Leadership: Practical Styles for Pastoral Ministry.* San Francisco: Harper and Row, 1987.

CHAPTER IV

Developing/Reviewing the Parish Mission Statement

A large urban parish in Houston, Texas developed a mission statement seven years prior to engaging in a workshop on developing collaborative ministry within the pastoral team. The facilitator discovered that the mission statement, which was no longer on public display, was locked up in a cupboard in the church. Only three members of the present pastoral team and forty-five of the current registered parishioners had been engaged in the formation of the mission statement. The parish mission statement was no longer commonly known or owned by the community. What replaced the large bronze plaque displaying the mission statement in the entrance to the church were photographs of the present pastor and all the previous pastors. This spoke volumes about the pastor's vision of who is important and how leadership is exercised within the local parish community.

The pastoral team spent a two-and-a-half hour session of the workshop discerning whether there was a need to engage in a review of the parish mission statement. The pastoral team were interested in reviewing the mission statement, while the pastor whose photograph replaced the mission statement was not in favor. This session of the workshop clarified that the pastoral team did not share the same vision of the church, which limited the development of communion within the pastoral team. When the pastoral team addressed the problem relating to the different visions of what the church is called to be, communication was improved, mutual respect and cooperation was fostered, and greater collaboration in ministry was manifest.

Collaborative ministry assists a parish in being more effective in its mission, and the process that combines an understanding of the ecclesiological, spiritual, and interpersonal dimensions of ministry with a pastoral plan of action adds to the overall effectiveness of a pastoral team. Each member of a parish staff has an individual perception of the ecclesiological, spiritual, and interpersonal dimensions of collaboration in a pastoral context. A process integrating these dimensions with a pastoral plan of action is needed if a group is to be effective as a pastoral team.

Parishes produce mission statements that often are rooted in the particular insights of the parish staff and are given credence by citing passages from the scriptures. In many cases the scripture citations are used as "proof texts" to support a particular subjective insight. The mission statement fashioned by the pastoral team and parish leadership often is ratified by the community. This process can easily fail to make incarnate the mission of the universal church within the parish. As a result, the mission statement of the parish becomes subjective, restrictive in its design, and unable to evoke commitment from parishioners.

The parish mission statement ought to be a local expression of the universal vision and mission of the church. The documents of Vatican II provide a solid foundation for creating a mission statement and developing a pastoral plan of action. The entire parish should be involved in (1) studying the Vatican II documents, (2) developing the parish mission statement, and (3) implementing the pastoral plan. This is a radical departure from previous procedures that began with the particular and subjective insights of a small group within the parish and then were promulgated among the wider parish.

This chapter provides a process of collaborative pastoral development and focuses on: (1) analyzing a collaborative process for developing a parish mission statement, (2) calling a parish assembly in which the parish amends the mission statement, (3) developing the spiritual life of the parish, (4) accepting and celebrating the mission statement, (5) discerning when to evaluate the mission statement, and (6) exploring a process for evaluating the mission statement.

The creation of a parish mission statement requires the active cooperation of all the baptized during the development of the mission statement and its implementation in a pastoral plan. The mission statement emerges from the shared reflection on the Vatican II documents by a large cross-section of parishioners. The mission statement focuses on key issues: celebration of the liturgy, education of all the baptized, social issues, development of the spiritual life of all, coordination of ministries, ecumenical commitment, development of a sound administration, and evangelization of the parish within the wider community. The vocation to be a people with a clear understanding of mission is further articulated in the development of a parish pastoral plan. The parish mission statement and its periodic evaluation require a commitment to engage in a reflective process that uses Vatican II as its bedrock. All the baptized participate in this discernment process, which creates a sense of ownership of the mission statement and encourages parishioners to be active during the development and implementation of a pastoral plan.[1]

Developing a Parish Mission Statement

The mission statement addresses three questions: (1) What are we called to be and do as a parish? (2) What steps can we take to become that kind of parish? (3) Is this vision of the parish an authentic expression of the universal church? Developing a mission statement enables the entire parish to become more of a community in which all the baptized are active in service (Jn 17:18; 20:21).

During a workshop I gave a pastoral team three different parish mission statements. Each mission statement was produced in a unique way: one was developed and written by the pastor without consultation, another was developed by the pastoral team, and the third was written by a committee after extensive parish consultation. The team were asked to identify which one was written by the pastor. No one in the group could identify the pastor's composition! The pastor who composed the mission statement on his own was skilled in pastoral theology, utilized appropriate concepts, and expressed in punchy sentences the vision of the parish. This exercise showed how easy it is to produce a mission statement that looks exciting and comprehensive on paper, but raises the question: "Whose mission statement is it, the pastor's or the community's?"

It is tempting for the leadership in a parish to short-circuit the process of consultation since this can be time-consuming and stressful. One urban parish spent two years engaged in extensive consultation with over five hundred small groups before producing their mission statement. At times people engaged in the small groups lost their tempers and struggled with defining their own call to mission and ministry, but the outcome of the process was a mission statement that was truly owned by the community. The consultative process provided the participants with an opportunity to experience Christ's presence among them. The five hundred groups engaged in study, reflection, and discernment of how they were called to mission and what it means to be church. This parish provides an invaluable model for all communities embarking on the process of developing a mission statement.

What process was used in your parish to develop the mission statement? How extensive was the consultative process?

The following model taps the wisdom of the community, respects people's skills and insights, and promotes the development of collaborative forms of ministry. In many parishes tension exists between the pastoral team and the pastoral council, and turf battles are not uncommon. Engaging in a process of developing or evaluating a parish mission statement provides an opportunity for deepening communion among all active in ministry and promotes healing of any conflict that exists between the pastoral team and pastoral council.

The pastoral team and parish council can share responsibility for (1) educating the parish concerning the development or evaluation of the mission statement, and (2) raising the consciousness of all the baptized to recognize their particular gifts and utilize them in building up the kingdom. This educational process provides information on the mission and ministry of all and gathers ideas, feelings, and convictions of parishioners in response to this information. This process enables all the baptized to be active in various forms of ministry. Parishioners are presented with ecclesiological, spiritual, and interpersonal formation that sustain the church as communion and facilitate collaborative ministry. All are responsible for the mission of the church and are called to minister to society.

The pastoral team collects statistical data about the local community that is integrated with information gleaned from the parish census.[2] This process identifies the needs of parishioners addressed by the development of the mission statement and explores the mission of the parish within the wider community.[3]

One parish in Italy asked me to assist them in the process of developing a mission statement. The pastoral team consisted of four lay ministers and a pastor; the pastoral council consisted of twenty-four members representing each ministry within the parish. The pastoral council worked in collaboration with the pastoral team to produce a mission statement. They decided to engage in extensive consultation with four goals: (1) to explore the pastoral needs being addressed by various ministries, (2) to identify the pastoral needs that the community was failing to address, (3) to provide a comprehensive parish profile, and (4) to use the data from the consultation as a bedrock for developing a parish mission statement.

Phase one of the consultation consisted of (1) the pastoral team developing a two-hour workshop that addressed the four goals by utilizing a needs assessment questionnaire, (2) the pastoral council implementing the workshop with the twenty-five groups active in parish ministry, and (3) the pastoral team processing the data gathered from the consultation. Phase two consisted of (1) each lay minister visiting ten households to complete a needs assessment questionnaire, and (2) the pastoral team and pastoral council processing the data which formed a foundation for developing a parish mission statement.

The planning, implementing, and processing the data from the needs assessment questionnaire by the pastoral team and pastoral council during the two phases of the consultative process promoted a deep level of trust between the pastoral team and pastoral council. The mission statement developed as a result of the extensive consultation was one that people were excited about since it was truly "their" parish mission statement.

How would your pastoral team and pastoral council respond to a similar process of collaboration? What pastoral need could your pastoral team and pastoral council address in a collaborative manner?

The parish should utilize at least two kinds of consultants to facilitate the development of the parish mission statement: a theologian who focuses on selected Vatican II documents, and a specialist in human development to train leaders in a small group process. The pastoral team and pastoral council identify individuals with leadership skills and invite them to attend a course on pastoral leadership. An invitation also is extended through the parish bulletin to other interested members of the community. The training consists of six two-hour sessions. The first three sessions focus on group leadership, the final three sessions focus on Vatican II. The pastoral team and parish council all participate in this formation program. The consultant in group process is responsible for training in various leadership skills: active listening, conflict management, and communication. The theologian works with the same leaders and focuses on the church's liturgical life, constitution, ecumenical expression, lay apostolate, missionary activity, and evangelization in the modern world. This equips the leaders with a deeper understanding of the universal mission of the church.

The pastoral council organizes the entire parish in home-based groups averaging ten participants. All registered parishioners receive a letter that (1) explains the process involved in developing a parish mission statement, (2) invites each parishioner to participate in this process by attending four two-hour meetings, and (3) offers each parishioner the choice of one of the Vatican II documents to be used in the group meetings.[4] The members of the pastoral council are among those trained in leadership who use the Vatican II documents in the small home groups to develop the parish mission statement. Each small group engages in (1) reading one of the Vatican II documents, (2) discussing its contribution to the mission of the universal church, and (3) articulating a draft proposal of the parish mission statement. Discussion groups require the services of trained and experienced facilitators and recorders. Every small group reports back to the pastoral team with its draft proposals. The pastoral team is responsible for collating the proposals for the parish mission statement and identifying the specific categories contained in the Vatican II documents. This composite picture gathered from the groups forms the rough draft of the mission statement.[5] Common needs which surface in many parish mission statements are: a more vital parish, a stronger sense of unity, a greater quality of community life, a deepened faith life, a greater involvement of all parishioners in ministry, a concern for ministry for those beyond the parish, more meaningful liturgies, Christian education for all ages, increased financial resources and facilities, greater integration of the variety of cultures, and concern for the youth.[6]

The entire parish refines, amends, and approves the parish mission statement by coming together at a parish assembly. Different forms of communication are used to invite parishioners to participate in this meeting: Sunday homilies, parish bulletins, letters to registered parishioners, and promotion by all participants in the house groups. During the week prior to the meeting, a team of parishioners extends telephone invitations to attend the parish assembly. The more people are involved in the planning and execution of this parish meeting, the greater the community's sense of ownership of the mission statement. The mission statement is a corporate expression of the pastor, religious, and parishioners and reflects the ideals and hopes of the wider parish.[7] During the parish assembly, parishioners share their common vision and mission of the parish and help to amend, refine, and then ratify the final version of the parish mission statement.[8] This meeting is collaborative in design, deepens the communion within the parish, and generates stronger commitment to implement the mission statement.

A Model for a Parish Assembly

The parish assembly begins with a short prayer session prepared by the parish liturgy group. The facilitator[9] then outlines (1) the format of the meeting, (2) the discernment process that created the rough draft of the parish mission statement, and (3) the consequences of ratifying the parish mission statement.[10]

7.30 p.m.–7.50 p.m.	Prayer/presentation of draft copy of the mission statement
7.50 p.m.–8.10 p.m.	Questions from assembly addressed to pastoral team: to clarify/make additions/express disagreement
8.10 p.m.–8.30 p.m.	Small groups (5–7 members) discuss suggested amendments
8.30 p.m.–9.10 p.m.	Feedback from groups: amendments/recommendations
9.10 p.m.–9.40 p.m.	Pastoral team present "refined" mission statement to assembly for approval
9.40 p.m.–10.00 p.m.	Prayer/acceptance of mission statement

The facilitator encourages the active participation of the general assembly in a manner that fosters openness, respect, and honesty (Mt 18:20). The assembly is reminded that all the baptized are equally responsible for promoting the mission statement and for fostering communion within the parish. The pastor concludes the deliberations by thanking the entire assembly for their collaboration in the discernment, articulation, and clarification of the parish mission statement. The meeting ends with a prayer prepared by the liturgy group wherein the mission statement is officially ratified. The assembly praises God for helping them in the discernment process, which fostered cooperation, increased collaboration, and created greater communion within the parish.

Celebrating the Acceptance of the Parish Mission Statement

The parish mission statement is displayed in the parish church at the Sunday eucharist following the parish assembly. The homily at all the liturgies focuses on key elements contained in the mission statement: the call of all the baptized to mission and ministry, the co-responsibility of all in building up the kingdom, and the communion that is generated through collaboration in ministry. The mission statement is promulgated in the parish in the Sunday bulletin in a letter to all registered parishioners, and on a poster for the various ministries, organizations, and school(s) within the parish. The various groups involved in ministry, each of the faith-sharing groups, and all parish organizations discuss the implications of the mission statement. How are we called by the terms of the mission statement to become more involved in creating a community where all are servants?[11]

The parish liturgy group prepares a liturgical celebration to take place one month after the initial proclamation of the mission statement. At this celebration the mission statement is officially accepted by the whole parish community. Representatives from the various ministries, organizations, and groups within the parish have a special role to play in this celebration. The tone is one of gratitude, joy, and thanksgiving. During the liturgy, a plaque outlining the nature of the mission statement is placed in a prominent place in the church.

The pastoral team coordinates all initiatives aimed at informing the parish about the mission statement. Written material is distributed to all parishioners, focusing on: the parish as a community of service where all the baptized are active in some form of ministry, the pertinent passages from Vatican II regarding collaboration in ministry, and reflection questions relating to mission and ministry.[12] The existing programs, e.g. RCIA, Re-Membering, scripture study, faith-sharing groups, and the various adult education initiatives, are provided with materials to foster a deeper understanding of the parish mission statement. All parishioners received materials that (1) foster the cooperation of all the baptized in ministry, (2) share responsibility for the mission of the church, (3) promote communion within the parish, and (4) facilitate the collaboration of all in building up the parish as a community of service.[13]

One parish took the mission statement it had developed and had it put to music. The community all learned the melody and memorized the words. The mission statement was sung during the liturgical celebration to mark the parish's acceptance of its call to be active in mission and ministry. All newcomers to the community were given a parish profile which manifests how the mission statement is being lived out in the various ministries within the community.

How were you first exposed to the mission statement of your present community? What could be done to promote greater awareness of the mission statement among the community?

Promoting Spiritual Growth Within the Parish

The faith life of the parish needs to be developed in order to implement the mission statement. Various renewal movements and renewal programs provide opportunities for faith development, e.g. Cursillo, Charismatic prayer groups, Focolare, Renew, Small Faith-Sharing Communities, and the Parish Evaluation Project. Yet these cater to the needs of a small percentage of parishioners. Every parishioner needs to be provided with extensive opportunities for faith development.[14]

One process that facilitates the spiritual growth of all is the collaborative planning and implementation of a spiritual formation week for the parish. The pastoral team appoints a renewal committee that is active in planning the spiritual formation week at least six months before the event. The renewal committee includes representatives of all groups and organizations active in ministry, plus other parishioners delegated by the parish team and pastoral council. The goals of the committee are (1) to collaborate in planning and implementing the spiritual formation week in the parish, (2) to experience a deeper sense of communion, and (3) to cooperate with a theological consultant to discern the qualities required by a suitable renewal team. The committee is responsible to the pastoral team and the pastoral council and provides progress reports to both.

The tasks of the renewal committee are planning the spiritual formation week, determining each committee member's role in the spiritual formation, and planning the follow-up to the formation week. The information gathered from the parish, which facilitated the writing of the draft copy of the mission statement, assists the renewal committee at its first meeting to explore potential themes for the parish spiritual formation week.[15] The second meeting begins with the renewal committee breaking into small groups of four to five. Their tasks: to explore topics, discern the needs of special groups in the parish, outline a possible schedule for the spiritual formation week, examine various options for discussion groups, and discern how best to publicize the event. The facilitator[16] gathers the large group together and summarizes the suggestions that emerged from each of the small groups.

The pastoral council searches for a formation team that can fulfill the spiritual needs discerned by the renewal committee. A search committee is established by the parish to interview and hire a formation team to facilitate the parish spiritual formation week.[17] The renewal committee consults with the pastoral team, pastoral council, and formation team to decide on the format for the week of spiritual formation in the parish, and the deadlines for specific parish activities, e.g. the program outline for the formation week and the publicity campaign.[18] The better the publicity, the greater the attendance at the formation week activities. The various groups active in ministry continue to use the parish mission statement as a focus for their prayer, reflection, and pastoral development. They provide valuable spiritual support for the renewal committee during the discernment process.

Long-range publicity for the formation week requires that all means of communication are utilized to invite the parishioners to participate in a parish assembly meeting. These different means of communication are supplemented by every member of the renewal committee "talking renewal" for months in advance. If feasible, the religious editor of the local paper interviews the formation team that will conduct the week-long spiritual formation. Short-term publicity consists of mailing each household a pamphlet describing the week's activities, speakers, and topics, together with a letter from the renewal committee inviting parishioners to attend. The week of spiritual formation is advertised in the diocesan newspaper and in other local parishes.

All members of the renewal committee speak to each ministry, organization, or group within the parish about the spiritual formation week. The formation team participates in the liturgies the week prior to the spiritual formation program and speaks at the end of each Sunday eucharist. Parishioners are invited to fast on the Friday before the formation week and to pray for its success. Details of the spiritual formation week are displayed in the church and parish facilities. Many parishioners are engaged in utilizing the various means of communication. Such cooperation utilizes the diverse gifts of the community and deepens the experience of communion within the parish.[19]

The program for the spiritual formation week addresses the diversity of cultures within the parish, educates all members of the parish regarding their call to ministry, and celebrates evening liturgies that will focus on living the Christian life. Group discussions take place after each service and focus on a spiritual foundation for collaborative ministry. The aim of the spiritual formation week is to promote an experience of communion within the church and enable all the baptized to utilize their gifts in the building up of the community.[20] The program is adapted to the particular needs of Hispanics, elderly, dedicated singles, young marrieds, youth, shut-ins, divorced and separated, alienated and children. The program for the formation week provides the entire parish with a common focus, increases cooperation, enables collaboration, and deepens communion.

The week of spiritual formation in the parish furthers the implementation of the parish mission statement by providing theological input and prayerful reflection upon the pastoral development in the parish. The renewal committee gathers two to four weeks after the formation week to evaluate it and explore possible ways to follow up. The renewal committee reports its findings to the pastoral team and pastoral council. An equal amount of energy extended during the planning of the spiritual formation week also is required during the follow-up period.

One parish renewal committee contracted a team in which I was a member to provide a week of spiritual formation. The team formed part of a community who specialized in evangelization and included a married couple, a single woman, a young man, a religious sister and a priest. We brought a diversity of gifts that made the formation week very attractive to the people who participated. The team was competent in collaborative styles of leadership, developing faith-sharing groups, utilizing small group process, and promoting consensus decision-making, and was skilled in spiritual direction, preaching, counselling and story-telling. The renewal committee developed the program in collaboration with the visiting renewal team which led to a diversity of needs in the parish being addressed. The parish also utilized the renewal team for the ongoing evaluation of the pastoral development within the parish.

What was your most enriching experience of spiritual formation? What does your parish presently need to enable all parishioners to be more active in living out their call to mission and ministry?

A Readiness To Evaluate the Mission Statement

The membership of many urban parishes is in a process of constant change. It is common for parishes to conduct an annual census by telephone to determine who is still resident within the community. I discovered through an annual census that thirty percent of the parish I was resident in changed every year. Given that the community was made up of over twenty-five hundred families, this created serious problems for parish development.

One evening I met with the RCIA team to plan the Sunday morning sessions for the coming month. While sharing our perceptions of various significant events we had celebrated in the community during the previous three years, one of the team could not grasp what we were talking about. Further discussion revealed that one of the ministers was not part of the community three years ago, and that approximately forty percent of current lay ministers were relatively new to the community. The time-span of the living tradition in the parish was limited to two years. The community had developed a very comprehensive mission statement, yet the high turnover of registered parishioners meant that very few of the current parishioners were conscious of the mission statement.

The community decided that it would engage in a process of reviewing the mission statement seven years after it was written. Yet this has never been attempted. My experience conducting workshops on developing collaborative ministry within parishes reveals that many parishes invest a large amount of time and energy in the consultation process culminating in the writing of a mission statement. Parishes often schedule a review of the mission statement in five to seven years, but few actually fulfill their plan to do so. Why is this pattern emerging? What are the reasons for parish mission statements being "cast in stone" once they are written?

Today most parishes have ongoing programs of adult formation, provide opportunities for children to prepare for the celebration of the sacraments of initiation, encourage liturgical planning and development, offer an appropriate program for the youth, and provide quality care for particular needs of different various groups within the parish community: the sick, dedicated singles, the unemployed, newly married, single parents, and the divorced. The average parish employs one or more full-time professional lay ministers who work in collaboration with the parish priests. In many cases the energy of the pastoral team is taken up with sustaining existing programs and training new ministers to share the role of spiritual leadership within the parish. Most professional lay ministers are currently exercising responsibility for many areas of development that are not listed in their job descriptions. The pastoral needs of people in our parishes are ever increasing, and people are asking assistance with their spiritual, psychological, and emotional development, expecting the pastoral team to provide some form of resolution. There is a high level of stress associated with membership of a parish pastoral team where there are constraints on time, energy, and available resources to address the expanding diversity of needs.

Attention, energy and resources are spent addressing the pastoral needs of groups that are vocal, articulate, and persistent. Each pastoral team needs to spend time discerning how the various programs offered to the community dovetail with the vision contained in the parish mission statement. It is vital for each pastoral team to spend quality time each year identifying the pastoral priorities and planning how to respond in an appropriate manner.

A pastoral team I worked with had recently completed the Renew program and were exploring the next stage of parish development. We spent three days together engaged in ongoing staff development. The most fruitful session focused on discerning whether developing a mission statement was the most appropriate means of continuing the involvement of many existing faith-sharing groups. The pastor and the rest of the team had different perceptions of future development. The pastor knew that he would be moved within the year and that the community would develop its mission statement. His concern was that his successor would disagree with the vision contained in the parish mission statement and would totally destroy it. Yet the pastoral team was conscious that after extensive consultation developing the mission statement, the community could truly own its mission statement. The pastoral team's task would be to inform the bishop of the ecclesial vision contained in the mission statement, which could assist the bishop to select an appropriate pastor who could enable the parish to realize the vision of church contained in the mission statement.

The pastor used the language of the parish "owning" the mission statement, yet he didn't believe that the bishop would select a pastor whose ecclesial vision matched that of the community's. This pastor's negative judgment of the bishop limited the possibility of the parish exploring the development of a mission statement. The pastoral team was excited about the possibility, but the pastor's view dampened the members' enthusiasm.

What experience of parish "ownership" has deeply impressed you? What needs to change in the present leadership style of the pastoral team to increase the parishioners' experience of "ownership"?

The pastor's vision and opinion on all matters of pastoral development carry immense weight within the pastoral team. Engaging in a process of identifying priorities, allocating resources, and developing appropriate programs for parish development demands a high level of maturity from all members of the pastoral team. A secure, skilled, and experienced lay minister can challenge the pastor's vision, his leadership style, and his spiritual competence, yet most pastors rarely experience such a challenge. In many pastoral teams the pastor gets what the pastor wants: for example, if the pastor sees the need for ongoing professional development for all members of the pastoral team, funding will be made available; if the pastor thinks that prayer is important, he will schedule prayer into pastoral team meetings.

In parishes there is a great deal of talk regarding "shared responsibility" and "consensus-decision making," yet many pastors are uncomfortable when their authority is challenged. One parish I worked with states in its mission statement: "We seek consensus-decision making in all pastoral matters," which really amused me since the mission statement in question was written solely by the pastor!

Transition is a way of life in many parishes today: entire areas experience significant demographic, economic, and social change. New pastoral problems are continually being identified: e.g. the ministry to AIDS sufferers, and the growing needs of the Hispanic community. There are frequent changes in parish personnel: pastors, associate pastors, and professional lay ministers are relatively free to leave parish ministry and utilize their skills and competence in new communities. In parishes which have a significant annual turnover in registered parishioners, there is a diminishing number of parishioners who are conscious of the origin and the history of the parish mission statement. The end result is that the mission statement becomes a decorative plaque hanging in the entrance to our churches.

Why is it that many parishes fail to engage in a process of reviewing or evaluating the mission statement?

The experience of one pastoral team casts some light on the problem. Their mission statement had been developed eight years ago. Currently there are only sixty of the three hundred parish members who were involved in the process of developing the mission statement still living within the parish. The pastoral team identified the benefits of reviewing the mission statement: "It is necessary in order to prevent perpetuating a narrow vision of the local church; the unhealthy perception of the parish at present is that we have nothing to do with the universal church, and one present danger is that we spend all the resources of the parish entirely on ourselves; a review of the mission statement would make the five thousand people who worship here more conscious of who we are as a community, and what we are called to be, and do." Yet the pastoral team really questioned *whose need* would be met by engaging in such a review or evaluation of the mission statement.

If a number of parishioners perceive that there is a real need to evaluate and review the mission statement, then they will participate in the process. But if the pastoral team members are the only ones who perceive this as being a valuable process that responds to a real need, they will be the only ones who are interested in working on the process of evaluating the mission statement. The key question that requires an answer is: *Whose need will be met by engaging in a process or reviewing/evaluating the mission statement?*

One reason many communities fail to engage in the evaluation of the mission statement is that there is no real perception or understanding among the vast majority of parishioners that engaging in the evaluation process will respond to a perceived need in the search for identity, belonging, and rootedness. The task facing the pastoral team is: (1) to educate the community regarding the historical development of the mission statement, (2) to identify the demographic changes and new pastoral initiatives developed within the parish since the mission statement was developed, and (3) to enable all to make the mission statement their own personal mission.

What commitment do you personally make in your ministry to realize the vision contained in the mission statement? What can the pastoral team do to promote the review/evaluation of the mission statement within the parish?

A Process To Evaluate the Mission Statement

All new parishioners who register in the community require an information package that provides a profile of the community, the various programs currently offered, the ministries currently available, the members of the pastoral team and pastoral council, a copy of the mission statement, and an outline of the projected pastoral development. In many instances the people engaged in ministering to new members of the parish community are amazed at the diversity of pastoral needs the parish currently addresses. All parishioners can benefit from an annual update of the parish profile.

When the pastoral needs within the parish community are not clearly identified the pastoral response is very limited. This problem can be overcome by electing someone to be responsible for improving communication within the parish, to identify all pastoral needs, and to collaborate with the pastoral team in developing a strategy to ensure that all pastoral needs are adequately addressed. This ministry of *communications coordinator* is responsible for ensuring that communication between the various ministries, pastoral formation programs, and organizations within the parish is a regular feature of parish community life. The communications coordinator is also responsible for reporting on how various groups and ministries are living out the call to ministry contained in the mission statement. Improving communications in the parish educates all members of the community regarding the universal call to mission and ministry.

The coordinator of communications[21] works closely with a committee selected from the membership of the pastoral team and pastoral council. Regular updates to these bodies ensure that the leadership of the parish are continually informed regarding current pastoral developments. The aim of the committee is to identify, explore, and suggest ways in which the parish can become a community where all are active in some form of ministry.

The communications committee utilizes the talents of all who underwent training in leadership skills and group process during the development of the parish mission statement. The pastoral council provides the committee with the lists of small groups who were consulted during the creative process. The communications committee invites all who were engaged in developing the mission statement to exercise a leadership function in new groups that will engage in the process of reviewing/evaluating the mission statement. It is the committee's responsibility (1) to gather information from all small faith-sharing groups, groups involved in various ministries, and people involved in parish organizations, (2) to process this information to provide a current annual parish pastoral profile to be communicated to the parish, and (3) to assist the pastoral team and the pastoral council to discern when is the appropriate time to engage in a process of reviewing/evaluating the mission statement.

One pastoral team invited me to assist them to promote greater ownership of the mission statement. The key to the process was promoting communication of the mission statement within the parish. The suggestions for raising consciousness in the parish included: "It should be translated into Spanish since the Hispanic community is expanding; the elements of the mission statement can be woven through the parish directory that is distributed to every household; all groups within the parish can use it to engage in an annual evaluation of their ministry."

The group found it a useful exercise to restructure the parish mission statement under the following categories.

Ecclesiology

—to strengthen bonds of friendship and hospitality that bind us to God;
—to foster unity with other faith communities;
—to serve the people in need;
—to do justice where there is inequality.

Spirituality

—to pray and celebrate in ways that foster the spiritual growth of a diverse community;
—to foster the faith development and renewal of all members in the various stages of the life cycle.

Leadership Styles

—to inspire community members to share parish leadership by developing and contributing their gifts;
—to improve pastoral care by nurturing and reaching out to individuals and families;
—to stand for human dignity and to promote peace.

Dividing the mission statement into these three categories enabled the pastoral team to appreciate the comprehensive nature of their mission statement. The pastoral team was able to explore "how" it is fulfilling the vision contained in the mission statement.

What benefits can you identify for your parish if it were to engage in a process of reviewing/evaluating the mission statement? How can our pastoral team create the appropriate climate for reviewing/evaluating our mission statement?

When the parish discerns that the time is ripe for reviewing or evaluating the mission statement it appoints a mission statement committee whose task is (1) to organize the small group consultation, (2) to plan the parish assembly, and (3) to arrange the parish celebration at which the community accept the "revised mission statement." This committee prepares materials for the three phases of the consultation: i.e. handouts for the group leaders, the program for the parish assembly, and the format for the parish assembly.

The first phase of the evaluation consists in:

(1)   communicating to the parish the nature and format of the evaluation process;
(2)   identifying leaders skilled in group process;
(3)   organizing a "sign up" Sunday where parishioners make a commitment to engage in the process;
(4)   scheduling the four meetings of the various small groups;
(5)   processing the data gathered from the small groups.

Each small group makes a commitment to meet four times weekly for two hours. The format of each meeting is:

7.30 p.m.–8.00 p.m.	Prayer/faith sharing
8.00 p.m.–8.20 p.m.	Presentation
8.20 p.m.–8.50 p.m.	Working in pairs
8.50 p.m.–9.10 p.m.	Large group feedback
9.10 p.m.–9.30 p.m.	Conclusion

The first session consists of analyzing the structure of the mission statement, breaking it into three distinct sections—I: Ecclesiology; II: Spirituality; III: Leadership Styles—and identifying the strengths/weaknesses of the mission statement. The second session focuses on exploring the ecclesial vision of the universal church and identifying the deficiencies of the parish mission statement. The third session investigates the nature of spiritual development and explores the call of the community to promote such development. The fourth session examines the prominent leadership style that is proposed by the mission statement and discerns ways in which leadership can be further developed within the community.

Phase one of the evaluation process concludes when the mission statement committee has collated and processed the reports from the various small groups, prepared an overview of the research conducted by the groups for the parish, and communicated the findings of the small group consultation to the parish.

Phase two of the evaluation process begins with the mission statement committee planning a parish assembly. The mission statement committee appoints a facilitator to be responsible for coordinating the parish assembly meeting. Three members of the mission statement committee each give one of the presentations on ecclesiology, spirituality, and leadership styles. The parish assembly is not restricted to those involved in phase one of the small group consultation, but is open to all parishioners. The format of the parish assembly meeting is:

Unit I

10.00–10.30	Session I—Presentation: Our Ecclesial Vision
10.30–11.00	Small Group Discussion
11.00–11.30	Large Group Feedback
11.30–12.00	Session II—Presentation: Spirituality
12.00–1.00	Lunch

Unit II

1.00–1.30	Small Group Discussion
1.30–2.00	Large Group Feedback
2.00–2.30	Presentation: Leadership Styles
2.30–3.00	Coffee Break

Unit III

3.00–3.30	Small Group Discussion
3.30–4.00	Large Group Feedback
4.00–4.30	Conclusion: outlining the final stage of the process of evaluating the mission statement

Each member of the mission statement committee who made presentations on ecclesial vision, spirituality, and leadership styles is assigned another member of the committee to collate the data gathered on the respective themes from the parish assembly. Each couple prepares a synthesis of the parish consultation focusing on ecclesial vision, spirituality, and leadership styles and reports this to the mission statement committee. The committee is given the task of writing a revised mission statement incorporating the findings from the small group consultation and the parish assembly.

Phase two of the evaluation process concludes when the mission statement committee has collated, processed, and communicated "the revised mission statement" (1) to each of the small groups engaged in phase one of the consultation, (2) to all participants of the parish assembly, (3) to all groups engaged in ministry, (4) to every parish organization, and (5) to all registered members in the parish community.

The final task of the mission statement committee is to organize a parish celebration at which the community ratifies "the revised mission statement." A format for the celebration is:

2.00–2.20	Prayer
2.20–2.40	Presentation of mission statement
2.40–3.00	Sung litany of praise thanking God for giving the community a call to mission and ministry
3.00–5.00	Parish picnic

The process of reviewing/evaluating the mission statement promotes communion within the parish and enables the community to truly "own" the revised mission statement.

Is your parish ready to engage in a process of evaluating the mission statement? What preparation is needed to educate the community regarding the benefits of reviewing/evaluating the mission statement?

Summary

The process used to develop and review/evaluate the parish mission statement utilizes the Vatican II documents. The extensive consultation utilized to develop/review the parish mission statement creates community involvement in ministry and ensures that the mission statement is an authentic expression of the universal mission of the church. This process facilitates greater cooperation, communion, and collaboration within the parish. All the baptized are engaged in developing the mission statement, identifying and developing their particular gifts, and utilizing their gifts in ministry. Many are engaged in the planning and execution of the spiritual formation week and are stimulated to fulfill the call to mission and ministry. Formation, support, and supervision in ministry animate more people to be actively engaged in ministry.

The entire process of developing and reviewing a parish mission statement is evaluated, including the effectiveness of the parish team and pastoral council as educators, ministers, and facilitators of the collaborative process. A collaborative process is employed to develop and to review/evaluate the mission statement, and to identify the areas of contention that hinder the development of the kingdom of God. The process is educational and helps to integrate ecclesiological, spiritual, and interpersonal dimensions of collaboration with the review/evaluation of the parish mission statement.

The pastoral team and pastoral council play a central role in this process: (1) fostering cooperation within the parish, (2) respecting the diversity of gifts and encouraging their use within the parish, and (3) building up communion by coordinating the reviewing/evaluating of the mission statement. Developing a mission statement and engaging in a process of reviewing the mission statement enables the parish to be a community in which all the baptized are active in mission and ministry, acting as leaven in the world.

Collaborative ministry is rooted in the understanding of the church as communion in which the entire people of God participate in the universal call to holiness, mission, and ministry. This process of developing and reviewing/evaluating a parish mission statement enables all to grow in holiness as they become more active in the mission and ministry of the church. Collaborative ministry calls all the baptized to communally express their priestly, prophetic, and royal ministry (1 Pet 2:4–5, 9–10),[22] to utilize their gifts in building up the ecclesial community, to practice mutual respect, and to participate in dialogue. Developing and reviewing/evaluating a parish mission statement based upon the Vatican II documents fulfills these goals.

Pastoral teams are committed to sharing responsibility with the community for the mission of the church. Those engaged in ministry seek to build up the kingdom of God, yet often they have (1) a different understanding of ecclesiology, (2) a limited spiritual foundation that fails to sustain all engaged in ministry, (3) diverse styles of leadership that hinder collaboration, and (4) a narrow experience of pastoral planning which limits the development of communion. These different perspectives are often hidden, are not addressed, and can lead to conflict in ministry.

How can the collaboration of all engaged in ministry be promoted? What kind of process can be utilized to address these areas of conflict and generate deeper communion?

A strategic planning process needs to be designed for all engaged in ministry that promotes communion and integrates ecclesiological study with theological reflection and pastoral development. What type of formation process can be designed for all engaged in ministry that seeks to integrate theory, reflection, and lived experience? For whom is this process designed? What does this process propose to accomplish, and with whom can it be implemented? How does the strategic planning process promote the cooperation of all engaged in ministry, deepen communion among all, and enable all to collaborate in building up the kingdom?

Chapter V responds to these questions and explores ways in which (1) the strategic planning process creates communion among all, (2) the planning committee utilizes consensus as a basis for all decision-making, (3) the gifts of all parishioners are utilized in the development of a strategic pastoral plan, and (4) the implementation of the strategic plan can be evaluated.

Reflection

1. The thing that struck me most about reviewing/evaluating the mission statement was . . .

2. I find myself resisting the process of evaluating the mission statement because . . .

3. What excites me about our current mission statement is . . .

4. The benefits I see in reviewing/evaluating our mission statement are . . .

Suggested Reading

1. Thomas P. Walters, *Handbook for Parish Evaluation.* New York: Paulist Press, 1984.

2. Gerard T. Broccolo, Susan C. Rosenback, Lucien T. Roy, and Lea L. Wolf, *Coordinating Parish Ministries.* Chicago: Department of Personnel Services, 1987.

3. Cynthia D. Scott, and Dennis T. Jaffe, *Managing Organizational Change: Becoming an Effective Change Agent.* Los Altos: Crisp Publications, 1989.

CHAPTER V

A Process for Strategic Planning

A diocese consisting of one hundred and ten parishes is currently involved in a parish-based pastoral planning process that evolved over the past three years. The process entitled "Companions on the Journey" promotes broad involvement in planning within every parish. The planning process is designed to identify the various pastoral needs, explore the available resources, and utilize the existing resources to maximum benefit for all. The bishop exercises the role of teacher outlining the ecclesial vision that forms the foundation for the planning process. The strategy involves meetings with each parish, with neighboring parishes, and with each of the six regions in the diocese. Each parish has a ten-member planning committee that acts in conjunction with the diocesan development committee. The planning committees work in consultation with the pastor, the pastoral team and the pastoral council. This extensive consultation process promotes greater sharing of responsibility for current pastoral needs and is currently exploring alternative models for exercising pastoral leadership in parishes.

The consultative process promotes communion, and makes incarnate the call of the community to fulfill the terms of the mission statement. The parish mission statement is a local expression of the universal mission of the church. The church's mission is to sanctify and evangelize society, acting as leaven in the world. Each parish is called to develop a pastoral plan of action based on its own mission statement as an expression of the mission of the universal church. The process of developing such a pastoral plan requires extensive consultation and the collaboration of all the baptized. Most people think that pastoral planning is something that exists only at the diocesan level. We are accustomed to seeing dioceses producing a five year pastoral plan which always looks impressive and comprehensive when we see the professional end-product in print. It is refreshing to discover a diocese that has engaged in broad-based consultation at the parish level that integrates the vision contained in the diocesan mission statement with pastoral development.

This chapter explores: (1) the significance of the strategic planning process; (2) the role of a planning committee; (3) the need to develop a mission statement; (4) the importance of identifying resources; (5) the methods of operation which integrate tactical decisions with the implementation of the strategic plan; (6) the development of performance indicators; (7) the monitoring of the implementation; (8) the evaluation of the strategic plan and the planning process; (9) the process for creating a forward plan.

The human body provides a useful image for understanding the pastoral planning process: the mission statement is like a skeleton; the pastoral plan forms the flesh; the extensive involvement of the parish community breathes life into the body. The pastoral planning process harnesses the talents of the pastoral team, pastoral council, all leaders of diverse ministries and parish organizations, and other skilled human resource consultants within the parish. All home-based groups that articulate and develop the parish mission statement are actively engaged in the process of developing a parish pastoral plan of action. Each home-based group is presented with an outline of (1) the ministries currently operative within the parish, (2) the initiatives of all parish organizations, (3) the resources available for pastoral development, and (4) the principles for setting goals and implementing objectives in pastoral planning.[1]

A Strategic Planning Process

The local church is called to be active in mission and ministry and requires effective management to fulfill this calling. Yet many parishes are plagued by internal problems in management practices. The difficulties experienced by the parish leadership are characterized by non-existent or inadequate goals and planning methods, budget and program over-extension, unsystematic, inaccessible, and untimely information systems for identifying and using human, financial, and material resources, top-heavy and rigid church decision-making structures which fail to adapt to changing circumstances, and committees and task forces which often lose sight of their mission and become reactive doers rather than planners and implementers.

These problems can be addressed by utilizing effective church management which focuses on careful and skilled planning. Planning is a theologically based discipline for thinking, equipping, and structuring the decision-making processes of the church that promotes effectiveness in the mission and ministry of the local church. Planning is a philosophy of responsible strategic decision-making in a complex and changing society. Planning is a theology with operational consequences: it enables the local church to learn how to become future-oriented; it is inherently open and tentative, yet is committed to implementing all goals and objectives.

One of the greatest challenges facing the local church is to engage in a process of strategic planning. Strategic planning is the process by which the parish leadership envisions the future of the parish and develops the necessary procedures and operations to achieve that future. This vision of the future state of the parish provides both the direction in which the parish should proceed and the energy to begin the move. The strategic planning process helps the parish to do more than *plan* for the future; it can help the parish to *create* its future. Yet it is more than just an envisioning process: strategic planning involves setting goals and objectives, and deciding on a time frame to achieve the future planned state. Targets need to be developed within the context of the future desired state of the parish and must be realistic, objective, and attainable.

The goals and objectives developed in the strategic planning process provide the parish leadership with a set of core priorities and guidelines that assist all day to day managerial decisions.

This model of strategic pastoral planning focuses on the process of planning which include a parish self-examination, the confrontation of difficult choices, the establishment of priorities, the implementation of the strategic plan, and planning when to begin the next planning cycle. Each diocese that engages in strategic pastoral planning provides a framework for each parish to identify needs, discern resources, and set goals to address the diverse issues within each community.

One diocese I consulted with in the midwest initiated a process of strategic planning sixteen years ago, and is currently initiating the fourth cycle of five year planning. The bishop used the following process during the first phase of planning: year 1—creating a task force to identify the ecclesial vision; year 2—developing a diocesan mission statement; year 3—initiating a plan to plan committee and conducting extensive consultation across the diocese; year 4—exploration of alternative models of parish leadership; year 5—development of a diocesan lay ministry institute.

The bishop together with the task force developed a clear vision of the local church and initiated the process of consultation which led to the development of a diocesan mission statement. The planning committee successfully addressed the critical questions that all groups engaged in strategic planning need to explore: How much commitment is there to the planning process? Who should be involved? How long will it take? What do we need to know in order to plan successfully? Who should develop the data? The diocesan planning committee explored the answers to these questions, clarified the expectations of ordained and lay ministers, and promoted commitment to the planning process by extensive consultation across the diocese. Projections of active clergy in fifteen years' time revealed that the diocese would experience a critical shortage of manpower. This apparent "crisis" helped all ordained and lay ministers to be open to alternative models of parish staffing.

The strategic goal of the first phase of the five year plan was to explore and make provision for alternative forms of staffing parishes. A key component in the success of the planning process was the visible commitment from the bishop and the task force to invest time, energy and resources to realize the ecclesial vision. One strategic decision the diocese made was to engage in the process of identifying, selecting, and forming lay leaders of parishes where there was no resident priest. The tactical decision that followed this was the development of a diocesan lay ministry institute. The bishop's high profile in the planning process from the outset promoted the development of a diocesan lay ministry institute which forms new leaders competent to respond to the "shortage of manpower" and collaborate effectively with the sacramental ministers.

What is your experience of diocesan or parish pastoral planning? What benefits/risks are inherent in the process of "strategic" pastoral planning?

The Planning Committee

Each diocese or parish that initiates a strategic planning process need (1) to identify who should be involved in the planning committee, (2) to identify and fully utilize the human resources available in the community, and (3) to solicit input and feedback from various ministries and organizations within the parish. To be effective the planning committee should not exceed ten to twelve permanent members. Various issues need to be addressed by the planning committee: How long will the process take? Do the leaders in various ministries have the necessary skills in group process and leadership styles to engage in planning? Is there consensus among parish leaders that now is an appropriate time to engage in planning? What resources can we call upon to develop the data necessary in the planning process?

The membership of the planning committee need to meet the following criteria in order to be effective:

—be informed regarding the local church and its development;
—be knowledgeable about the members and demographics of the parish community;

—have an established record of creative leadership within the parish that is
    recognized by other members;
—possess knowledge of business planning;
—be committed to making priority time to the planning process;
—be free from other conflicting parish commitments.[2]

The planning committee has the following goals: (1) to introduce the theology, values, theory, and methods utilized in planning to the leadership of the parish; (2) to provide ongoing formation in the planning process for all parish leadership groups equipping them with the necessary skills to engage in planning; (3) to integrate and assimilate the discipline of planning into the mission and ministry of the church.[3]

The planning committee meets every two weeks during the first stage of the process which lasts six months during which it formulates the strategic plan. It is responsible for the process of developing or evaluating the parish mission statement to be endorsed by the wider community, the development of strategic plans, and the testing, integration, and implementation of the action plans. The planning committee is evaluated at regular intervals by a separate independent body, e.g. an external consultant, or a task force from a neighboring planning committee. The planning committee conducts its meetings off-site away from the interruptions of daily work. A center used for team-building sessions provides a suitable environment that is conducive to the kind of envisioning and confrontation that is involved in strategic planning.

Strategic planning in a diocese or parish has a direct impact on budgeting. The strategic planning schedule should be established so that the results of the planning process can be fed directly into the budget considerations for the coming year. My experience in providing formation with parish personnel is that most parishes fail to allocate adequate financial resources for ongoing professional development. A critical factor in the decision to engage in strategic pastoral planning is the provision of an appropriate budget.

One midwest diocese I visited impressed me with the way in which it budgeted for its strategic planning process. The bishop with the planning committee decided that the success of the strategic planning process hinged upon providing two professional full-time consultants for each of the six regions in the diocese. The funding needed to resource twelve new members of the Diocesan Office for Pastoral Development was made available. The twelve professional diocesan consultants were employed to provide (1) training regional facilitators in small group process and leadership skills, (2) formation in communication and management skills, and (3) supervision of facilitators engaged in the pastoral planning process. Two consultants were permanently allocated to each of the six regions in the diocese and were required to address issues surrounding the closure or merger of parishes, and to explore alternative models of parish leadership. The impact these consultants had on the pastoral development across the diocese was colossal.

The provision of adequate financial resources is critical for pastoral development at both the diocesan and the parish level. The commitment of a diocese, region, or parish to pastoral development is visible in the percentage of the annual budget assigned to ongoing training, formation, supervision and evaluation.

If diocesan funding were made available to your parish, how could the pastoral team enable the parish to be more effective in strategic planning?

Developing a Mission Statement

The mission statement provides a foundation for developing the goals and objectives of the strategic plan. The planning team addresses the following concerns when engaging in the process of developing a mission statement: (1) What are we called to be and do as a diocese and as a parish? (2) What steps can we take to become that kind of parish? (3) Is this vision of the parish an authentic expression of the universal church?

The responsibilities of the planning committee include: (1) fostering cooperation within the parish; (2) respecting the diversity of gifts and encouraging their use within the parish; (3) building up communion by coordinating the reviewing and evaluation of the mission statement. A process for developing a parish mission statement and discerning when to review or evaluate the mission statement is outlined in chapter IV.

Statement of Resources

The first formal step in diocesan or parish strategic planning is initiating a process to identify the resources of the community. Resources in this context are closely associated with the values held by individuals and communities: e.g. a pastor who values innovation as an important personal value will envision a different future for the parish than a pastor who holds security as a high personal value. The personal style of a member of the pastoral team can have a significant impact on the rest of the team: e.g. a counselor who holds confidentiality as a personal value can enable the entire team to assume the value of confidentiality. Similarly, if the majority of the pastoral team hold maintenance more than mission to be a value, then the parish becomes a community which is focused on maintenance of current programs and ministries. When a value becomes broadly accepted, even though it may not be held as a parish value, the implementation of all pastoral plans is affected. The task of the planning team at this stage is to identify what happens to organizational values within the parish, acknowledge the present trend, and address the related issues when considering implementation of the strategic plan.

Strategic planning promotes (1) the clarification of values and the identification of resources among parish leaders and the parish as a whole, and (2) the development of consensus between individual ministries within the community. The strategic planning process advances the planning committee's vision and supports commonly held values.

Twelve years ago the local bishop in a small rural diocese decided that a priority diocesan value was the development of modern means of communications. The importance and value of developing sound communication systems was evident in the bishop's tactical decision to expand the number of personnel employed in communications, which resulted in the reduction of personnel in other diocesan offices. Today this small diocese is currently offering a comprehensive manual of audio/visual resources to promote the development of lay ministries in its own diocese, and offers its resources to many larger dioceses across the country. The pace of pastoral development in that diocese has been accelerated by the use of diverse modern means of communication.

The value that the bishop gave to communications was evident in the time, energy, funding, and human resources he provided for the diocesan office of communications. Sharing his vision, using all available means of communication, led other pastors and pastoral associates to appreciate the pastoral value of communications. The more people who own a particular value, the easier it is to make it incarnate within the organization. Each parish holds organizational values which need to be identified in the process of pastoral planning. Once the individual values of the pastoral team have been worked through, the values held in common by other parish leaders need to be identified. The values held in common by the parish community are organized and manifested in the programs and ministries offered by the parish. The planning committee is responsible for identifying the series of assumptions underlying the way leadership is exercised and ministry functions within the parish. The planning committee keeps a record of organizational assumptions and explores them during this first phase of strategic planning.

The parish culture is made up of the pastoral team's values, the organizational values of the parish, the parish's philosophy of ministry, the available resources, and its operating assumptions. The parish culture guides all involved in parish organizations and ministries in the decision-making process and the completion of various pastoral initiatives. The parish culture is evident in the physical setting of the parish church, grounds, and parish office. The rites, rituals, and stories told of heroic members of the parish form pieces of the jigsaw that help to identify the parish culture. The strategic plan must be integrated with the parish culture; otherwise it is doomed to failure. The strategic planning committee examines its own culture to identify how this affects the process of planning the future of the parish community.

The most important, yet most difficult part of the planning process is developing an index of parish resources that analyzes all individuals, groups, organizations, and ministries within the parish that will be affected by the development of a strategic plan. The planning committee identifies the significant leaders in the community who will be affected by the strategic plan and explores how the strategic plan affects their status, freedom of action, and relationships?[4]

The planning committee is responsible for raising the parishioners' consciousness of a system of values which can help a parish become more flexible and self-renewing. This new style of church management has several characteristics, qualities, and behaviors which form a comprehensive system for ongoing pastoral development. Strategic planning:

—is experimentally inclined;
—acknowledges error, embraces uncertainty in order to learn;
—establishes goals as a way of identifying what the local church needs to learn;
—seeks and uses new knowledge;
—builds and supports its systems around innovators.

Resistance to these new ways of operating are to be expected. Strategic planning in a diocese or parish can create anxiety and uncertainty which some leaders will find intolerable. Consequently the planning team can expect three patterns of resistance to change: (1) a denial of the need for change, (2) a rejection of the proposed process of planning, and (3) a failure to provide adequate support systems and skilled facilitators to promote a change in the behavior and values of the parish. The planning committee needs:

—to identify and choose from a variety of desired possible futures for the parish;
—to relate the parish to the local community in pursuit of its chosen future;
—to develop and implement planned action steps which lead to the realization of the chosen future;
—to develop the internal management system needed in order to achieve its chosen future.[5]

Diocesan curia and parish pastoral teams that do not understand the nature, goals, and objectives of strategic planning fail to initiate a process that promotes effective pastoral development. The strategic planning process is badly conceived when members of the planning committee are incompetent and unable to address the complex issues surrounding pastoral development.

A diocese in Italy made a request for eighty thousand dollars to a foundation to finance a two year assessment of all types of religious formation in the diocese. The foundation invited me and another consultant to evaluate the proposal and explore how best the funding could be used to promote ecclesial development. The three hour consultation with the Office for Religious Formation revealed significant problems in communication: (1) the director of the Office for Religious Formation failed to inform or collaborate with colleagues regarding the proposal; (2) the religious education staff was misinformed regarding the reason for the consultation with the foundation—the members thought that they were attending a finance meeting, and were angry with the manner in which the proposal for funding was developed; (3) the presumption was that a two year research project identifying the diocesan needs for religious formation would provide the raw data upon which a pastoral planning process could be built.

We provided the diocese requesting funding with (1) an overview of the nature, purpose, methodology utilized in the pastoral planning process, (2) a critique of the proposed two year research project, and (3) an alternative strategy for pursuing pastoral development in the diocese. The diocese was not given the funding it requested, yet the bishop and Religious Formation Office were grateful to the two of us for identifying the problem, evaluating the proposal, and offering an alternative strategy for development. The director of the Office for Religious Formation neglected (1) to consult his staff regarding the proposal for funding the two year research project, and (2) to engage his staff in a process of completing a values audit. The end result was that conflicting strategies for development were proposed during the consultation. Consequently, the Office for Religious Formation in the diocese revised its strategy and received funding after submitting its revised proposal.

When have you been involved in identifying resources? What benefits can you identify for diocesan offices and pastoral teams to compile an index of resources?

Methods of Operation

The planning process utilized in a diocese or in parishes involves making both strategic and tactical decisions. What are the decisions that need to be taken? What type of decisions are being taken? The impact of making a strategic decision in the parish will be felt for many years: e.g. the decision to build a new pastoral center adjoining the parish church. This strategic decision will affect the parish budget for many years; it may curtail the development of new programs, and will have consequences for employing new personnel to maximize the use of the new facilities. Strategic decisions have enduring effects on the parish which make them difficult to reverse. Hence it is important that church leaders understand the significance of making strategic decisions before they implement them.

Strategic planning is concerned with formulating the parish's goals as well as determining the policies which will influence the choices of the means to achieve the goals. Strategic decisions focus on the "what" questions ("What shall we do?"). Tactical planning is concerned with selecting the means by which to pursue a specified goal—within the policies which have been made. Tactical decisions tend to deal with the "how" questions. Having decided to build a parish pastoral center, how shall we go about raising the necessary funding? Strategic planning is broad in scope: tactical planning is narrower.

Strategic decision-making has four foci:

1 Purpose   Decisions are made regarding who we are as a parish, what we are called to be about, and where we intend to go, and the results we desire from being committed to ministry and mission.

2 Operational Dynamics   Decisions are made regarding the quality of life within the parish, the leadership styles that are utilized, the patterns of influence, the expected levels of performance, and how to effectively utilize the gifts of the community while engaging in mission and ministry.

3 Resources   Decisions are made regarding the resources required to reach the planned destination determined through the setting of goals, the selection and training of skilled leaders, the generation and management of the funding required for the development, and the facilities and equipment integral to the planned development.

4 Structure   Decisions are made regarding the nature of the work to be undertaken, the organization of the work into manageable units, the discernment of sufficient work groups, their linkage, and the creation of policies to guide their decision-making process.[6]

A diocese contracted me to provide a critique of their pastoral strategy for development. I spent four days interviewing the twenty key personnel responsible for various diocesan offices. The best case of strategic and tactical decision-making I have investigated had been implemented by the leadership of the Office for Pastoral Council Development. After extensive consultation with other diocesan offices the director of the Office for Pastoral Council Development made a strategic decision: *each parish pastoral council was to become the body responsible for pastoral planning within the parish.*

Three years prior to my visit the strategic decision had been taken to enable pastoral councils to assume this comprehensive function. The tactical decisions that had been implemented included (1) identifying the need for pastoral councils to assume this new role, (2) sharing the vision of this "new role" for parish councils with other diocesan offices, pastors, and lay ministers, (3) developing the resources to enable parish councils to be effective in their new role, (4) training of facilitators to implement the strategic goal in all regions in the diocese, and (5) testing, evaluating, and improving the resources in several pilot schemes, and making these resources readily available to all pastoral councils.

The director of the Office for Pastoral Council Development has integrated the organizational development with the provision of human and financial resources utilizing a suitable structure for ongoing formation. All parishes interested in developing the pastoral council as the pastoral planning group in the parish are utilizing a home-grown diocesan manual which promotes prayer, pastoral formation, and the development and refinement of personal skills, and sharpens the group skills needed to engage in pastoral planning.

The strategic decision to develop the pastoral council as the body responsible for pastoral planning is being effectively realized through appropriate implementation of tactical decisions.

What has been your best experience of strategic and tactical decision-making? How has it helped you in your present ministry?

Integrating Tactical Plans   The planning committee works in liaison with the pastoral team to integrate the development and integration of tactical plans. These two bodies are co-responsible for informing the community regarding the implementation of tactical plans.

One pastoral team engaged me to do a workshop designed to evaluate the implementation of their tactical plan. Each member of the pastoral team was responsible for a particular area of ministry: e.g. liturgy, social concerns, youth, religious education. But the offices for the professional lay ministers on the pastoral team and the offices for the clergy were several blocks apart. The strategic plan involved building a pastoral center, incorporating the existing church complex, to accommodate all members of the pastoral team in a suite of offices and provide adequate meeting space for the expansion of ministries and programs. The new facility enabled the pastoral team to be more available to each other for consultation, support, feedback, and social contact.

The planning committee provided the raw data for the tactical plan by (1) identifying the plans for extending the programs offered to the parish, (2) outlining the material, physical, and human resources available for the pastoral development, (3) allocating the necessary funding for the improving current ministries, and (4) evaluating the current phase of implementation. The data revealed a discrepancy between a collaborative vision for the various ministries and the failure to realize the tactical vision by fully utilizing the new parish pastoral center.

The tactical plan explored during the workshop aimed at reducing the discrepancy between "vision" and "reality" by addressing (1) the transition of many home-based programs and groups, e.g. the religious education program, to fully utilize the new facilities for their meetings, (2) the tension between the "office staff" and the pastoral team created by greater exposure to one another in the new facilities, and (3) the high level of stress experienced by members of the pastoral team created by developing and implementing new programs in response to expanding pastoral needs.

What tactical plans has your pastoral team implemented that have promoted greater collaboration in ministry?

Implementation of Plans   Every parish has a strategy for pastoral development that is often implicit, yet is not thoughtfully examined. The process of strategic planning outlined in this chapter enables the pastoral team to make strategic management an explicit reality. Strategic management involves the execution of an explicit strategic plan that is consistent with the values and beliefs of those engaged in the process of pastoral development.

The final stage in a strategic planning model is implementation, yet the pastoral plans cannot be implemented until integration and checking occur. There is a continual need for implementation throughout the planning process: e.g. if the values audit reveals conflicting values among parish leaders, these need to be addressed as soon as the problem is identified; the parish mission statement should not be accepted unless there has been a process of extensive consultation resulting in consensus regarding the content of the mission statement.[7]

One pastoral team invited me to address a critical problem experienced during the implementation of pastoral plans. Conflict and confrontation arose because three different value systems focusing on the process of consultation were currently operative: one member believed in selective consultation, another in comprehensive consultation, and a third in a combination of the previous two. The pastoral team's failure to reach consensus regarding the nature of consultation led to the unavailability of vital information required to make tactical decisions. The workshop explored how to address the different value systems, reach consensus regarding consultation in the community, and be more effective in the planning process. The pastoral team had struggled with the problem of conflicting values for the previous two years, and were grateful that the workshop increased their competence in the planning process.

The planning committee has an important function: to identify and gather information relating to the implementation of the strategic plan, and to make periodic reports to the parish focusing on pastoral developments and the current state of the consultative process. All available means of communication are used to announce and present the strategic plan to the parish community. A parish assembly is a useful means of communicating the strategic plan to the community. The entire parish is invited to participate in a parish assembly in which the proposals, goals, and objectives of the pastoral plan are explained and ratified.[8]

The parish assembly meeting lasts two and a half hours and utilizes the following format:

2:00–2:40	Session I: Presentation of strategic pastoral plan; clarify goals/objectives
2:40–3:05	Session II: Small groups of five to seven; discuss/explore one facet of the strategic plan
3:05–3:45	Session III: Large assembly; feedback
3:45–4:15	Session IV: Approval of strategic plan
4:15–4:30	Liturgical celebration[9]

The planning committee is responsible for informing the parish about the strategic pastoral plan. The pastoral plan is displayed in a prominent place in the church, presented to every parish organization and ministry, shown in the parish school(s), and sent to every household in the parish. The pastoral plan aims to develop the parish as a community of service. All the baptized are called to be active in some form of ministry.[10]

The implementation of the strategic plan is handed from the planning committee to the pastoral team. The most important test of implementation is the extent to which the pastoral team and leaders of ministries integrate the strategic plan into their everyday tactical decisions. When the initial response from a leader in ministry confronted by a decision is to consider whether an answer can be found in the parish planning process, then strategic planning is a reality. Once a strategic plan is operative it becomes a template against which parish decisions are made, the scale on which resources are allocated, and the foundation for developing all ministries.

What experience of implementing pastoral planning do you value most? What made this development such a memorable experience for you?

Contingency Planning The strategic planning committee is required to identify opportunities that promote pastoral development, as well as potential threats that can thwart the implementation of strategic planning.

One pastoral team in Texas was anxious about the change of pastor that would take place during the following six months. The outgoing pastor had a comprehensive vision of church, was competent in management skills and group process, and was active in the development of collaborative forms of ministry within the parish. The pastor, associate, and pastoral team were all concerned that the "new pastor" would not share the vision of church or have the necessary skills to sustain the current phase of pastoral planning. I challenged them to accomplish the following tasks: (1) to identify the vision of church upon which the pastoral development has been founded; (2) to provide a profile of the spirituality that sustains all ministries and organizations active within the parish; (3) to outline the leadership styles operative within the pastoral team and pastoral council; (4) to identify ways in which the mission statement and strategic and tactical decisions will influence pastoral development over the next two years; (5) to outline an ecclesial vision and the management skills that the "new pastor" needs to possess to exercise spiritual leadership in their community. This data should be presented to the personnel board and the bishop to help them discern who the new pastor should be.

The pastoral team was skeptical whether the personnel board and the bishop would pay attention to such a profile during the selection process. However, I pressed them to be pro-active in the process of selecting a new pastor and to do their part to ensure that a suitable candidate would be found for the position.

Having gathered the pertinent data for the personnel board, the pastoral team was able to make contingency plans focusing on how to initiate the new pastor and collaborate with him during the first year of his tenure. Since the pastor can promote or hinder strategic pastoral development, it is vital that all pastoral teams make such contingency plans.

Contingency plans need to be made for (1) the replacement of key members of the pastoral team and the group leaders of all key ministries, and (2) the modification of demographics which can affect parish income and limit the available funding for programs that develop ministries.

What has been your experience of making and implementing parish-based contingency plans? What ministries in our parish could benefit from making contingency plans?

Monitoring

The purpose of monitoring is to establish the extent to which the mission statement and the goals of the strategic plan have been implemented. Monitoring includes collating information from other dioceses and parishes focusing on the degree to which they are successfully implementing their strategic goals. For monitoring to be effective, data pertinent to the development of the strategic pastoral plan is collected, analyzed, and evaluated.

I spent several months engaged in monitoring during the spring of 1991, traveling around eleven dioceses in the United States. My objective was to gather pertinent data that is vital for initiating a strategic pastoral plan for a diocese. My research revealed that (1) the professional lay ministers employed in most diocesan offices have developed excellent resources for promoting the development of lay ministries, (2) all diocesan offices are willing to freely share the resources they have developed, (3) most diocesan offices have undergone a reconfiguration during the past five years which resulted in a reduction of personnel that slows down the sharing of resources, (4) all were interested in sharing the vision contained in current pastoral developments in other dioceses, and (5) few diocesan offices were aware that they were often duplicating resources developed by other diocesan offices.

There is a real need for more pro-active networking across dioceses aimed at sharing the vision of pastoral development, exploring strategies for church development, and making available to other dioceses the current pastoral programs and resources. In the process of conducting performance audits in different dioceses I became a broker of information and resources. The diocesan personnel in each diocese I consulted with were excited about the possibilities of pastoral development and about the volume of "unknown human and material resources" I made readily available to them.

One important function of the planning committee in each diocese or parish is to identify and gather the available resources for implementing the process of strategic planning. Time spent in examining the performance of other parishes and dioceses, networking with key personnel in pastoral development, and exchanging resources is mutually enriching and realizes communion.

What is your experience of monitoring? What are the benefits and the drawbacks of the practice?

Evaluation

The purpose of evaluation is to compare the data generated during the monitoring with the goals of the strategic decision process. The evaluation tests the extent to which the strategic decisions have been implemented. For an evaluation to make sense it is necessary to formulate performance indicators which evaluate the planning committee and the strategic pastoral plan. The performance of the planning committee can be measured by direct feedback from the pastoral council and diverse ministries and organizations affected by the planning process.

A process is created to evaluate how the strategic plan is being implemented.[11] One year after celebrating the acceptance, initiating, and implementing of the strategic plan, the planning committee and pastoral team (1) determine any major changes that have occurred within the parish, (2) make the necessary contingency plans, and (3) evaluate themselves as educators, ministers, and facilitators of this collaborative process.[12] The findings of this discernment process will be communicated to all parishioners at a parish assembly meeting.

The mission statement and pastoral plan provide the central focus for the evaluation. The following key questions are addressed: Are the mission statement and pastoral plan viable and practicable? Are they realistic at this time, given the resources available to the parish? How many parishioners are aware of the mission statement? Does the wider parish share the goals and objectives enunciated in the pastoral plan? What major changes have affected the parish during the preceding year? Are the parish team and pastoral council successfully ministering to the needs of the parish community? In what ways does the parish support those engaged in ministry?[13]

The planning committee is evaluated on how effectively it has educated the parish about the mission statement and facilitated the implementation of the pastoral plan.[14] The planning committee assists the pastoral team in evaluating the need for additional expertise to fulfill its ministry, and if additional expertise is warranted it seeks to employ the necessary personnel. The evaluation process highlights how implementing the strategic plan has enabled all to be active in sharing their faith and become engaged in ministry. Each parishioner is invited to respond to a questionnaire that addresses the parish's awareness of the mission statement and pastoral plan, the opportunities provided for their spiritual growth, and the challenge extended to all to utilize their gifts in ministry. Are particular ministerial needs being adequately met, including the needs of youth, elderly, and single-parent families? Are lay leadership and ecumenical dialogue growing? Is hospitality being extended to all in the parish? Is there a growing experience of communion among various ministries, groups, and organizations? Do the social justice and adult education programs promote collaboration in ministry? Do the interpersonal skills and leadership styles exercised by the pastor and the parish team empower collaborative ministry? The planning committee collates the responses to this questionnaire and meets with the pastoral team to provide mutual evaluation, support, and feedback.[15]

The purpose of the evaluation process is to learn from past experience and prepare better for future commitments. The members of the planning committee also are evaluated by the community they serve. How effective have they been in facilitating greater cooperation, collaboration, and communion within the parish?[16] The coordinators of the various ministries distribute evaluation forms to all those engaged in ministry. These forms provide a basis for evaluating the planning committee and pastoral team as educators, ministers, and facilitators of collaborative ministry. The various groups active in ministry complete the evaluation forms and present them to the pastoral team. The pastoral team uses this information to communicate with the planning committee and evaluate how both have exercised their stewardship.[17]

A diocese in Canada engaged me as a consultant to evaluate the integration of fourteen diocesan bodies into a new organization called "The Office of Pastoral Personnel." My task was to review and critique the nature, goals, and objectives of the new Office of Pastoral Personnel which affected the lives of six thousand lay ministers. The document was produced by one of the assistant bishops and a task force from the priests' council. During my research and evaluation of the new office, I attended a day of formation for the diocesan lay ministry institute. At the end of the meeting there was a public outcry from participants since they first learned of the existence of this new office from an article in the local newspaper published the previous day. This new office makes policies for all professional lay ministers and permanent deacons relating to selection, training, hiring, wages, sickness plan, retirement scheme, and termination of contract. It was clear from the lay ministers' outrage that the task force from the priests' council had created the new office without consulting those affected by the new policy.

The director of the institute informed the angry assembly that I could speak about the document. I stood up and stated: "Not only do I have a copy of this document but I have been asked to critique it—if anyone would like to have some input please see me before 2:00 P.M. tomorrow when I present my critique to the bishop." Several people immediately took up the offer and met with me after the meeting. The document had several deficiencies: (1) the task force had failed to consult those engaged in formation for lay ministry and permanent diaconate; (2) there were no annual evaluations of the new office; (3) the design of various committees showed that an unfair advantage was given to the French speaking community; (4) the theology of ministry contained in the document was outdated.

The following day the bishop was presented with an eight page critique of the document, which included numerous footnotes on the theology of ministry and a process for an annual evaluation of the new office. The bishop was delighted with the proposed amendments and stated that the amended document was more comprehensive. Subsequently a copy of the amended document was mailed to the bishop with a copy to the director of the lay ministry institute. The critique of the nature, goals, and objectives of the Office of Pastoral Personnel prevented a major schism between the ordained and six thousand lay ministers in the diocese. The diocesan leadership learned through the experience that an evaluation process is vital for effective strategic planning. The strategic vision becomes a reality when all pastoral programs are exposed to some form of annual evaluation.

The parish is conscious of itself as a community called to minister to society and to act as leaven in the world. The goal of the strategic plan is to empower the parish to become a community in which all the baptized are active in ministry. There is a growing consciousness that by virtue of baptism all are called to be ministers and to receive ministry. There is a developing understanding of pastoral ministry as occurring in everyday life, not merely in liturgical ministry, and a growing awareness that all are called to minister to society.[18]

One diocese I consulted with had developed a diocesan pastoral plan using a planning committee in each parish. I spent three days exploring the strategy, development, and implementation of the consultative model used in the planning process. Research revealed that there was a discrepancy between the strategy outlined in the parish planning manual and the way in which the consultative process had been conducted. The discrepancy in the strategy was that the clergy had not been consulted during one of the critical phases of the pastoral planning process. The planning committee had been engrossed in developing the materials and training facilitators for phase four of the pastoral plan, and they overlooked consulting the clergy during this important stage of planning and development. I was able to overview the entire process, highlight the discrepancy, and enable the planning committee to address the problem during the next stage of implementation. The development appraisal keeps the planning process from floating off in an unguided or misguided direction.

How effectively does your pastoral team evaluate parish programs? Do you engage in an annual evaluation of pastoral planning?

Forward Planning

Scheduling is vital to strategic planning, and is the process by which time requirements are established for each program currently offered to the community. When used effectively, scheduling (1) fulfills the objectives of the pastoral plan with a minimum degree of conflict, (2) identifies who does what and by when, and (3) combines the time-phasing of each objective to other objectives. Effective scheduling starts at the end point of the planning horizon and works backward to the initial step, thinking through and testing each individual step of the program. The amount of time, energy, and resources needed for scheduling depends on the complexity of the overall strategic plan. Scheduling may require a heavy investment of research and experimentation, or may simply be a case of deciding the appropriate time frame for completing a particular program.

Forward planning cannot be implemented without adequate scheduling wherein the identified needs of the community and the gaps in the current implementation of the plan are addressed. The scheduling process illustrates the long-term aims of the pastoral plan and is itself in need of ongoing regular evaluation. One criteria for evaluation compares the degree in which the master calendar reveals the maximum accomplishment of objectives by the planning committee, the pastoral team and the pastoral council, with the minimum degree of conflict.[19]

Two critical areas of concern explored during the forward planning stage are: (1) Are we doing things right? (2) Are we doing the right things? The planning committee identifies the strengths, weaknesses, opportunities, and threats presented by the data gathered while addressing these two questions.

An environmental analysis responds to the question "Are we doing things right?" in pastoral development. The parish planning committee assesses each program, the human resources currently available, the financial capital available for formation and supervision of ministries, and the physical assets available for implementing each program. The environmental analysis also responds to the question: "Are we doing the right things?" by focusing attention on parish demographics, the evolving needs of the community, the direction of various programs, and the available resources for ongoing development.

The planning committee addresses the following questions: (1) What does the future hold? (2) How do we best respond to the future? (3) What threats exist in the external and internal environment? (4) What opportunities are presenting themselves? (5) What future do we wish to create? (6) What resources are needed to cope? Conducting an environmental scan enables the planning committee to identify which goals and objectives of the planning process are on target or behind schedule, and to clarify where refinements need to be made to the strategic plan.

Summary

The diocese or parish that engages in strategic planning is able (1) to envision the future of the parish, (2) to provide the direction for pastoral development, (3) to harness the resources necessary to realize that future, and (4) to create its desired future. Strategic planning is experientially inclined, acknowledges uncertainty, learns from its mistakes, establishes goals, seeks and uses new knowledge, and builds its support systems around innovators. Selecting a competent planning committee is vital to the process of strategic planning. The members of the planning committee are required to be creative leaders within the community, to be experienced in local demographics, and to be capable of investing priority time in the planning process. The goals of the committee are to explore the ecclesiology, values, theory, and methods utilized in the planning process, to provide training for leaders of various ministries in planning skills, and to integrate the discipline of planning with the terms of the mission statement. The planning process includes the formation of a parish profile, the development of a parish mission statement, the discernment of strategic and tactical goals and objectives, the provision of an appropriate budget to implement the strategic and tactical decisions, the managing of a performance audit, and an evaluation of the planning process. Strategic planning is concerned with formulating the goals of the community and determining the policies that provide the means to achieve these goals.

The planning committee's first task is to compile an index of parish resources and audit the values of the leaders of the community. Commonly held values are manifested in the programs and ministries offered by the parish. An index of parish resources analyzes all organizations and ministries affected by the planning process and explores the impact on values, status, freedom of action, and internal relationships. Strategic planning clarifies the values of the parish and promotes consensus between individual values and community values. The planning committee examines the parish culture and its own culture to identify how they influence the decision-making process and to heighten the consciousness of the community regarding the operative values which empower the parish to create its desired future.

The planning committee addresses various patterns of resistance to change: a denial of the need for change, a rejection of the proposed process of planning, and a failure to provide skilled facilitators to promote change in behavior and values of the parish.

The planning committee and pastoral team share responsibility for the implementation of the pastoral plan. The strategic plan is implemented to the extent that the pastoral team and leaders of various ministries integrate the strategic objectives with everyday tactical decisions. The evaluation of the planning committee and pastoral team by the community they serve focuses on (1) their effectiveness in educating the community about the mission statement, (2) their competence in promoting the implementation of the pastoral plan, and (3) their proficiency in generating cooperation, collaboration, and communion within the parish. Such an evaluation process advances consciousness of strategic planning, increases the level of accountability, and develops commitment within the community to create its desired future.

What type of formation process can be utilized to increase commitment to collaborative models of pastoral development? How can the collaboration of all engaged in ministry be further promoted and coordinated? A process needs to be designed that integrates the spiritual, interpersonal, and developmental components of ministry within the context of a common vision of church.

Chapter VI responds to this pastoral need and explores a workshop that promotes collaboration in ministry among diocesan offices, pastoral teams, pastoral councils, small basic ecclesial communities, and all engaged in formation for ministry. The workshop entitled "Developing Collaborative Ministry Within the Parish" is designed (1) to identify the competence of participants currently engaged in collaborative forms of ministry, (2) to explore the root causes of resistance to collaborative models of ministry, and (3) to enable the participants to assume responsibility for addressing the critical areas of resistance.

Reflection

1. My most significant learning on strategic planning is . . .

2. What excites me about strategic planning is . . .

3. The benefits to be gained by entering a strategic planning process are . . .

4. To engage in strategic planning our pastoral team needs to . . .

Suggested Readings

1. Paul M. Deitterich, *Practical Guide to Church Planning.* Chicago: The Center for Parish Development, 1981.

2. J. William Pfeiffer, Leonard D. Goodstein, and Timothy M. Nolan, *Shaping Strategic Planning.* Glenview: Scott, Foresman & Co., 1989.

3. Archdiocese of Milwaukee, *Walking Together: Collaborating for the Future.* Milwaukee: Steering Committee for Parish Planning, 1991.

CHAPTER VI

A Model for Ecclesial Development

Parish pastoral teams which implemented a workshop on "Developing Collaborative Ministry Within the Parish" stated that some things they liked best about the workshop were:

—it became a tool for us to engage in self-reflection and evaluation of the collaborative way of being Church;
—the opportunity to brainstorm, explore new ideas, and get excited about possibilities;
—I was able to share faith (not just programs) with other staff members;
—I could see and feel God's presence within each person's ministry during the reflection times and group discussion;
—the sharing one-on-one and the large group reflections enabled us to experience communion.

Many parish pastoral teams engage in a process of ongoing formation and staff development. The amount of money allocated for staff development in the parish annual budget reflects the extent to which the parish is committed to ongoing training for its professional leaders. Ongoing formation programs that enable individual ministers to explore key issues in developing collaborative ministry are to be encouraged at the parish, diocesan, and national level. The national organizations for various ministries offer annual conferences focusing on pertinent areas of human, spiritual, psychological and ecclesial development. Many parish ministers take advantage of such conferences to network with other professional ministers and refine areas of pastoral competence. There is also a need for all members of parish pastoral teams to engage in workshops that promote the development of communion within the pastoral team itself.

Collaborative ministry is rooted in the image of the church as communion in which all the people of God participate in the universal call to holiness, mission, and ministry. The whole church shares responsibility for its mission and ministry. All the baptized are called to participate in the salvific mission of the church and contribute toward communion in the church. Collaboration in ministry assists the promotion of the gospel and fosters communion.

This chapter examines the grounds for utilizing a workshop on "Developing Collaborative Ministry Within the Parish" and focuses upon (1) the rationale behind the workshop, (2) the preparation required to implement the workshop, (3) a methodology for development, and (4) the role of ministries.

Collaborative ministry calls all the baptized to a communal expression of their priestly, prophetic, and royal ministry, to a use of their gifts in building up the ecclesial community, to mutual respect, and to participation in dialogue. Collaborative ministry can empower the church to be more effective in its mission, and can be initiated within the context of a reflective process that combines an understanding of the ecclesiological, spiritual, and interpersonal dimensions of collaboration with a pastoral plan of implementation. The pastoral team, pastoral council, and many others engaged in ministry in the same parish often have vastly different understandings of the ecclesiological, spiritual, and interpersonal dimensions of collaboration. There is a need for a theological foundation that can facilitate collaborative ministry.

The Goal of the Workshop   The workshop is designed to address this diversity in ecclesiology and implements a process that enables pastoral teams, pastoral councils, small basic ecclesial communities, and all engaged in formation for ministry (1) to understand the doctrine of Vatican II and post-conciliar teachings regarding collaboration in the church, (2) to develop an appreciation of a collaborative style of spirituality, (3) to explore the interpersonal skills and leadership styles that facilitate collaborative ministry, and (4) to integrate the above dimensions in a local parish mission statement and pastoral plan for collaborative action (Appendix A).

The Format of the Workshop   The workshop consists of five two-and-a-half hour sessions. The five sessions explore the following topics:

> **Session I:** The ecclesiology of communion presented in Vatican II, the 1985 Extraordinary Synod of Bishops, and John Paul II's *Christifideles Laici,* which provide a foundation for collaborative ministry.

> **Session II:** A model of spirituality that facilitates communion and empowers collaborative ministry.

> **Session III:** The leadership styles that promote communion and foster collaborative ministry with a focus on training, evaluation, feedback, and supervision.

> **Session IV:** The ecclesiological, spiritual, and interpersonal concepts that promote communion; the integration of these concepts with the parish mission statement facilitates collaborative ministry.

> **Session V:** The integration of these same concepts with a collaborative model that promotes communion among all engaged in ministry by developing a pastoral plan for the parish.

The five sessions of the workshop are designed to be implemented in various ways (Appendix C): (1) over a three-day residential period, (2) during five consecutive weeks, (3) three half-day meetings one week apart, or (4) two units involving an overnight stay followed by an all-day session one month later.

The Rationale Behind the Workshop

Those engaged in ministry often have different perceptions of ecclesiology, spirituality, leadership styles, and pastoral planning. These foundational differences are frequently not articulated, not understood, and therefore not addressed. This lack of awareness often causes conflict among those active in ministry. This workshop addresses these problems by (1) enabling all ministers to articulate their ecclesiological foundation, spiritual heritage, leadership style, and experience of pastoral planning, (2) revealing significant areas of conflict, and (3) exploring how reviewing a parish mission statement and developing a pastoral plan of action can foster cooperation, collaboration, and communion.

Each of the five sessions of the workshop utilizes an adult education model that creates a lived experience of communion and helps develop collaborative ministry within the parish. Sessions one through three have the same format: presentation (35 minutes); two reflection questions based on the presentation (25 minutes); sharing in pairs focusing upon the two questions (25 minutes); large-group sharing (40 minutes); conclusion (25 minutes). Sessions four and five have a similar format: exploring the parish mission statement/pastoral plan in the large group (30 minutes); two questions to facilitate sharing in pairs (30 minutes); presentation (30 minutes); two reflection questions (30 minutes); large-group response to the two questions (30 minutes).

Session I, entitled "An Ecclesiological Foundation for Collaborative Ministry," utilizes the ecclesiological vision of Vatican II and provides participants with a solid ecclesiological foundation for collaborative ministry, insight into how ecclesiological vision is incarnate in many areas of ministry, and an indication of the challenges that collaborative ministry presents to all engaged in ministry. Ministry is seen as a result of baptism in which the whole church is called to assume responsibility for its mission and ministry. The focus is on the common and ordained priesthood working together to build up the kingdom, which results in an increase in collaborative forms of ministry.

The leaders of a formation community I worked with in the midwest struggled to reconcile different visions of what we are called to be as church. The group lived together, planned courses for academic, spiritual, and pastoral development, and evaluated the formation program. During the first session of the workshop, I discovered that one member of the staff had a very traditional and hierarchical understanding of the church, while the rest of the staff favored a more collegial and participatory model of church. The tension created by the different ecclesial models adopted by the group had not been addressed: judgments had been made, opinions hardened, and a safe distance observed. The first session of the workshop addressed this problem by inviting the group: (1) to reflect on the question "What is my ecclesial vision, and how is it evident?"; (2) to share their responses in pairs; (3) to feed their sharing into the large group. The large group sharing helped to resolve many areas of tension: the opinions condemning the more traditional ecclesial model were dropped, a healthier respect for different visions of ministry emerged, and greater bonding between the entire staff evolved. One effect of the first session was that the staff member who held a traditional vision of church shared openly during the meal, and stayed to enjoy the chat afterward. During the previous six months he had never shared one evening meal with other staff members. This first session of the workshop raises the participants' consciousness of how vital the connection is between our vision of the church and how we live out this vision in every aspect of our ministry.

Session II, entitled "A Spiritual Foundation for Collaborative Ministry," promotes a communal spirituality in harmony with the ecclesiology of communion presented in Vatican II. It provides participants with a spiritual foundation that facilitates collaborative ministry, an awareness of Christ's presence in the individual and the community, an understanding of the conditions for establishing the presence of Christ among all engaged in ministry, and an appreciation of how to develop the spiritual growth of all. This spiritual foundation is designed to produce greater cooperation, co-responsibility, and communion among the whole people of God.

A pastoral team that implemented the workshop had recently taken two new staff members on board. During the second session participants shared their responses to the question "What can I do to ensure that the Lord is always present when we meet as a parish staff?" Suggestions from the team included: to respect each person, recognize his or her dignity, and believe that God is present in him or her; to be emotionally and spiritually as well as physically present during our meetings; to pray for our team all week long, interceding in an intentional way; to be gentle in word and action when we hold each other accountable; to be conscious that God is present especially when issues that engage us emotionally are discussed; to do a better job at affirming each other. The sensitive way in which the team responded to this question enabled all to share their faith at a deep level, increased the level of trust within the team, and promoted communion between new and older members of the team.

Session III, "The Leadership Styles That Facilitate Collaborative Ministry," reveals tensions that exist between proclamation and praxis, and examines the processes involved in promoting communion and collaboration within the parish framework. This session provides participants with the organizational models that promote collaboration in ministry, the leadership qualities necessary for collaborative ministry, the exercise of power and the resolution of conflict that facilitate collaborative ministry, and the feedback, supervision, evaluation, and training required for developing collaborative ministry.

A group of lay ministers who were near completion of their formation program in California were fascinated by this session on leadership styles. Discussion with the group revealed that the faculty actively promoted a "collaborative vision" of ministry, yet failed to model this vision in their teaching methods. For example, the faculty contracted me to implement the workshop on collaborative ministry, but were not willing to include those in the formation program, nor those engaged in the administration of the program. The end result was that the entire workshop was duplicated: one week with the student body, the second week with the faculty, with the administration being entirely neglected. When I presented my final evaluation to the faculty a similar dichotomy emerged: Each of the faculty received the final report, but there were serious doubts raised regarding presenting each of the student body with a copy. The evaluation highlighted the discrepancy between professing to utilize a collegial model of leadership while operating out of a more hierarchical model of leadership.

Session IV, entitled "Developing/Reviewing the Parish Mission Statement," examines how the universal mission of the church is articulated within the local parish. This session integrates ecclesiological theory and theological reflection with pastoral development, and utilizes the Vatican II documents to stimulate reflection wherein the pastoral praxis of the parish is evaluated. Participants are given the opportunity to analyze various processes utilized to develop a parish mission statement, to identify common needs addressed by parish mission statements, and to explore a method for developing or reviewing the parish mission statement. All the baptized are engaged in developing or reviewing the parish mission statement, identifying and developing their particular gifts, and utilizing their gifts in ministry.

A pastoral team in Colorado had developed a parish mission statement seven years ago. They responded to the question "How can we as a community review our mission statement?" Possible proposals included: (1) to utilize the five speakers already contracted to facilitate the program for adult formation; (2) to train more facilitators in leadership skills and group process; (3) to review the mission statement over a three year period engaging all groups, ministries, and organizations within the parish; (4) to complete the review process with a parish assembly that will mark the fortieth anniversary of the parish. The pastoral team was convinced of the value of reviewing the mission statement, and was eager to initiate the process.

Session V, entitled "Developing a Parish Pastoral Plan," highlights the limited implementation of pastoral planning in parishes and provides a collaborative process in which all the baptized can participate in the articulation and development of goals and objectives for pastoral action. This process is designed to promote communion within the community and to provide participants with the opportunity to explore how to promote the spiritual growth of all in the parish, to discern the role of the coordinator of ministries, and to integrate the parish mission statement with a pastoral plan of action.

A parish planning committee had developed a comprehensive pastoral plan. My task was to review and evaluate the implementation of the strategic goals and tactical decisions created by the planning committee. The strategic goals for the next five years included: (1) to strengthen parish stewardship of human, fiscal, and organizational resources, (2) to strengthen the faith of the community through evangelization and outreach, and (3) to enrich bonds with

the larger community. The consultation with the planning committee identified the goals that had been realized: to change the role of pastoral team from
schedular to trainer, to increase community involvement in seasonal planning,
to develop a re-membering program, to provide more opportunities for inter-
committee collaboration, and to develop policies and procedures for the use of
new facilities. The goals that had not been realized included: (1) to integrate
members of the non-English speaking community, (2) to design a process for
evaluating programs, (3) to develop an ecumenical program, and (4) to clarify
the relationship between the new mission statement and the strategic goals. The
consultation provided an overview of what is currently happening in the community, outlined who is engaged in what ministry, and clarified long-range and
yearly goals and priorities.

Preparing To Utilize the Workshop

Advance communication is needed to promote participation in the workshop.
Those interested are informed of the critical areas that will be addressed in the
workshop, the necessity of collaborative ministry, and the benefits of educating
the community regarding participating in a workshop on "Developing Collaborative Ministry Within the Parish." A leaflet containing an outline of the purpose, aim, commitment, and structure of the workshop is distributed to interested parties (Appendix A). A meeting is organized to inform the participants of
the goal, format, rationale, methodology, and preparation required to implement the workshop.

All groups interested in participating in the workshop are required to participate in a process of mutual discernment before establishing a contract (Appendix B) with the facilitators.[1] All interested groups are required to review the
qualifications, skills, and experience of the facilitators, to complete the initial
workshop questionnaire, and to interview the prospective facilitators. The following format is useful for the discernment interview:

I   **Facilitators**—affirm how the group is effectively collaborating in ministry;

                    —identify issues that hinder collaboration in ministry [based on the findings of the initial workshop questionnaire]. (Appendix E) (20 minutes)

II   **Group Leader**—facilitates discussion focusing on the needs and expectations of the group to be more collaborative in ministry, the collaborative strengths and weaknesses of the group, and the skills needed to promote greater collaboration. (20 minutes)

(prospective
participants)

III   **Dialogue**—addresses the state of readiness of the group, the ability to address root causes of resistance to collaboration, and the competence of the facilitators.[2] (20 minutes)

Any group wishing to utilize the workshop appoints a coordinator to inform the facilitators within two weeks of the group's decision to establish a contract.[3]

Each participant is asked to prepare for the workshop by studying suggested readings (Appendix D). The main source is *Grass Roots Pastors: A Handbook for Career Lay Ministers* by Leonard Doohan. This author provides an ecclesiological foundation for collaborative ministry, highlights critical issues in working together, and provides practical exercises for developing the faith of all engaged in ministry. *The Church as Communion* by Michael A. Fahey supplies insight into the "Ecclesial Community as Communion." A spiritual foundation for collaborative ministry is offered in *From Scripture to Life* by Chiara Lubich, and diverse ways of praying are outlined in *By Way of the Heart* by Wilkie Au, Loughlan Sofield and Brenda Harmann provide a process for developing a mission statement and creating a pastoral plan in *Developing the Parish as a Community of Service*. The archdiocese of Milwaukee presents a parish-based planning process in *Walking Together in Collaboration*. These readings assist participants in their preparation for the workshop and seek to expose participants to the central themes of the workshop, to provide a common focus for discussion prior to participating in the reflective process, and to assist each minister in his or her formation for collaborative ministry. The coordinator will contact the facilitators to inform them of the issues raised in the five sessions of group discussion based on the suggested readings.

The background readings are chosen to complement the five presentations in each session of the workshop and are most useful when they are read prior to each of the five sessions. The reflection questions contained in each of the five sections of the suggested readings are carefully designed to assist the participants to articulate and share their experience of ecclesiology, spirituality, leadership styles, and pastoral planning, and to promote a living experience of cooperation, collaboration, and communion.

Each group preparing to participate in the reflective process meets five times to discuss and reflect on the suggested readings.[4] Each group selects a facilitator and presenter for each of the five sessions and engages in the following process:

I   **Presentation**—overview of the suggested readings focusing on the challenges and opportunities presented by the material. (10 minutes)

II   **Reflection**—two questions to reflect on and respond to in writing. (10 minutes)

III   **Sharing**—sharing answers to the reflection questions in pairs.[5] (20 minutes)

IV   **Large Group**—large-group feedback focusing on positive and negative responses. (20 minutes)

The initial workshop questionnaire (Appendix E) is completed before the five sessions. Each of these five sessions focuses on the major themes of the workshop and is designed to provide the facilitators with (1) an appreciation of participants' training and experience in ministry, (2) the participants' perception of ecclesiology, spirituality, leadership styles, and pastoral planning, and (3) an awareness of critical issues that may need to be addressed during the workshop. The coordinator meets with the facilitators after the third preparatory session to present the facilitators with the participants' responses to the questionnaire and an overview of the issues raised by the suggested readings. This provides valuable information for the facilitators as they prepare to implement the workshop.

A deanery pastoral council in Indianapolis that implemented the workshop seriously addressed the suggested readings. They utilized the above process and presented me with a clear outline of the deanery pastoral council's views on ecclesiology, spirituality, leadership styles, and pastoral planning. The reading, reflection, and discussion among the council during the five preparatory meetings highlighted areas of consensus and contention regarding collaborative ministry. These issues were able to be properly addressed during their annual retreat when they implemented the workshop over a three day period.

Each group implementing the workshop is asked to complete an initial and a concluding workshop questionnaire which utilize a "Likert scale" and consist of thirty statements, questions, and open-ended assertions. A "T-test" is used to measure the initial workshop and concluding workshop scores on the above categories, which reveals the candidates' perception of change and agreement in regard to ecclesiology, spirituality, leadership styles, and pastoral planning.[6]

Significant data is available from implementing the workshop with diverse groups of ordained and lay ministers in parish pastoral teams, deanery pastoral councils, and formation communities. A comparison of the initial workshop questionnaires with the concluding workshop questionnaires reveal:

Ecclesiology   The lay ministers score higher than the ordained ministers, yet the concluding questionnaires reveal that the ordained ministers manifested the greater change in perception at the end of the workshop.

Spirituality   The ordained ministers scored higher than the lay ministers, yet the lay ministers' change in perception was greater.

Leadership Styles   The highest score and the greatest change in perception in all four categories is apparent from the ordained ministers response to the statement "Conflict and confrontation need to be addressed in order to facilitate collaborative ministry."

Pastoral Planning   The ordained ministers' change in perception was greater than lay ministers' change in perception in seventy-five percent of the questions. Yet results from this category highlight that ordained and lay ministers are neither experienced, skilled, nor competent in the process of pastoral planning.

The final open-ended statement manifests a significant change in perception in all groups that participate in the workshop. At the conclusion of the workshop the participants manifest a competence (1) to identify where collaborative ministry already exists, (2) to share a common ecclesial vision and further develop communion within their respective ministries, and (3) to address the attitudes that create conflict and confrontation, and hinder the development of collaborative ministry.[7]

The workshop on "Developing Collaborative Ministry Within the Parish" provides a model that can be utilized by diocesan, deanery, and parish pastoral councils, diocesan curias, pastoral teams, individual ministries (e.g. liturgists, ministers of religious education), Renew groups, basic ecclesial communities, presbyteral councils, faculty and students engaged in seminary formation, and all preparing for ministry. It provides participants with an opportunity to identify their different perceptions of ecclesiology, spirituality, leadership styles, and pastoral planning, to discover the root causes of tensions between those engaged in ministry, and to promote better communication, cooperation, and collaboration in ministry.

The workshop is most effective when it is implemented in a collaborative design in which the participants represent a cross-section of ordained and lay ministers. Experience reveals that such a combination increases collegiality, mutuality, and accountability among all ministers engaged in the mission of the church.

The Methodology Contained in the Workshop

Participants are presented with the pertinent theory on developing collaborative ministry by studying the suggested readings prior to each session and responding to the thirty-five minute presentation during each of the five sessions. Participants are to reflect on the theory contained in the readings and presentations by keeping a journal, responding to the two reflection questions during each of the five sessions, and sharing their reflection in pairs, as well as within the large group. Participants deepen their understanding of pastoral praxis during the workshop by exploring the benefits and risks of reviewing a parish mission statement and developing a strategic pastoral plan. This process is designed to integrate an ecclesiology of communion which facilitates collaborative ministry with a communal spirituality that promotes communion and the leadership styles that sustain communion within a parish. This approach is designed to empower participants to be more skilled in developing collaborative ministry within their parish.

The facilitators seek to integrate the roles of educator and minister in the workshop on "Developing Collaborative Ministry Within the Parish." The duties of the facilitators include: (1) meeting groups interested in implementing the workshop; (2) outlining the nature, structure, and purpose of the workshop (Appendix A); (3) helping the participants fill out the initial workshop questionnaire (Appendix E); (4) preparing the presentations for each of the five sessions (Appendix F);[8] (5) studying the experience of previous participants;[9] (6) conducting the five two-and-a-half hour sessions; (7) recording the responses of participants to the reflection questions; (8) completing the concluding workshop questionnaire and workshop evaluation (Appendix E).

Responding to the question "What I liked best about the workshop" participants stated:

—the opportunity to enter a reflective process with the pastoral team using an effective process;
—the opportunity to share the vision of collaborative ministry and dialogue about our leadership style(s);

—the realization that I must work with the team in order to build communion;

—the chance to know each other better and to share our faith;

—the knowledge that we can provide support, supervision, feedback, and evaluation for one another.

The facilitators prepare for implementing the workshop with the group who have established a contract by:

—reviewing Chapters I through V which provide the basis for the five presentations (Appendix F);

—reviewing the experience of other groups that utilized the process;[10]

—processing the data gathered from the initial workshop questionnaire;

—discerning the best possible schedule for implementing the workshop (Appendix C).[11]

The final session of the workshop concludes with the participants' evaluation of the facilitators and the reflective process utilized in the five sessions. The following process has proved useful:

I   Participants complete the concluding workshop questionnaire and the workshop evaluation. (Appendix E)   (15 minutes)

II   Facilitators affirm the areas in which collaborative ministry exists, highlight the root causes of conflict and confrontation that are preventing greater collaboration, and invite the group to address one of these issues in the coming year. (15 minutes)

III Establishing a goal that addresses an area of resistance to collaborative ministry and mutually discerns the value of a six-month review process. (15 minutes)

The facilitators are responsible for processing the data gleaned from the evaluation instrumentation, comparing the results of the initial workshop and concluding workshop questionnaires, identifying the different perception of change recorded by the ordained and lay ministers, preparing a report outlining the areas of significant growth in collaborative ministry as well as the areas of most resistance, and meeting with the coordinator of the group to discuss the findings.

The final session of the workshop concludes with the facilitators identifying the root problems that hinder the development of collaborative ministry, enabling the group to take responsibility for addressing the issues that cause conflict and confrontation, and offering to help participants address particular areas of resistance to collaborative ministry.[12]

My most fruitful evaluation session was held with the director of a lay ministry institute one week after the final session. The director was provided with (1) a series of bar graphs contrasting the participants' change in perception in ecclesiology, spirituality, leadership styles, and pastoral planning before and after the workshop, (2) a report identifying the significance of the changes in perception in all four categories, and (3) a synopsis of the root causes of resistance to collaborative ministry. The director took notes during the exchange, met with his faculty to process the findings, decided on their strategy for addressing the areas of resistance, and established a contract for a follow-up meeting with me six months later.

The facilitators meet the participants six months after the workshop to evaluate the progress in individual formation and group process, and to focus on the critical areas left unaddressed. A review process enables the participants to identify progress in addressing the areas of resistance to collaborative forms of ministry. A sample schedule is:

Reevaluation

9:00–11:30	Session one: reviewing progress made in an area of resistance to collaborative ministry
11:30–12:30	Lunch
12:30–2:30	Individual consultation with the facilitator
2:30–5:00	Session two: discerning how to promote ongoing formation and the development of skills necessary for collaborative ministry
5:30–6:30	Liturgical celebration

Session one focuses on the progress made in the critical areas since the workshop: reconciling different ecclesiological visions, analyzing the spiritual formation program, training in leadership skills, and identifying formation and resources available for pastoral planning. Session two focuses on the identification of current needs that are not presently addressed and outlines a process wherein individuals and groups can address these perceived needs. This review process builds in accountability and offers the possibility for support, supervision, feedback, and evaluation for all engaged in collaborative ministry.

Utilizing the Workshop: Projected Development

The workshop improves cooperation, promotes communion, and develops collaborative ministry among all. The greater the number of participants engaged in implementing the workshop, the greater the number of people actively promoting communion and cultivating collaborative ministry.

A fall publicity campaign promotes awareness and interest of parishioners and invites a commitment to participate in the workshop. A brochure is distributed to all households, groups engaged in ministry, and parish associations and committees. The brochure outlines the goals and objectives of the workshop, provides an overview of the format and design, and indicates the benefits that previous participants experienced. Information evenings are organized monthly during September through November to utilize a similar reflective process utilized in the workshop to promote collaborative ministry, to educate all regarding the challenges and benefits of collaborative ministry, and to encourage commitment to the vision of creating a community of active disciples.

One possible format of the workshop that promotes cooperation, increases collaboration, and deepens communion among the wider community is Schedule V (Appendix C). This format could be used during October to implement the workshop with the parish leadership, e.g. pastoral team, pastoral council, leaders of particular ministries, small scripture and faith-sharing groups, and parish associations. The following strategy is designed to educate the wider parish concerning the ecclesial foundation for collaborative ministry and to integrate theological reflection with pastoral praxis that promotes collaborative ministry:

Year I Fall	Parish leadership implements the workshop: two overnight stays/one month apart
Lent	Parish-wide implementation: one session each week of Lent
Pentecost	Parish leadership retreat: matching perceived needs to available resources; setting priorities
Year II Fall	Parish assembly meeting/home-based groups: set goals/objectives for coming year that promote collaborative ministry
Pentecost	Parish planning committee retreat: review implementation of goals/objectives
Year III Fall	Reevaluation of goals/objectives: parish assembly meeting/home-based groups[13]

Members of the parish are encouraged to participate in the workshop during Lent. Cross-fertilization is encouraged among all ministry groups, organizations, associations, and interest groups, e.g. adult children of alcoholics, divorced and separated people, newcomers, and single adults. One format that fulfills the goals of the workshop invites a small group of eight to ten participants to meet over an extended period of weeks, with adequate time for studying the suggested readings and engaging in theological reflection. The normal format for implementing the workshop would be small groups of eight to ten participants, meeting one evening during each week of Lent. The parish leadership is employed in the Lenten implementation as facilitators for the small home-based groups. The Lenten implementation concludes with each small group identifying the areas in which collaborative ministry is operative, recognizing various attitudes that hinder the development of collaboration—e.g. conflicting ecclesiologies, a lack of spiritual formation, a need for training in leadership skills—and discerning the priority in which these perceived needs are to be addressed.

The parish leadership spends an overnight Pentecost retreat, setting priorities regarding the perceived needs, identifying the available resources, and setting goals and objectives for the coming year. A consultant[14] is contracted to facilitate the gathering. One possible format is:

Friday	7:00–9:30 p.m.	Session I: Identification of perceived needs
	9:30–11:00	Social interaction: Informal discussion with facilitator
Saturday	9:00–11:30	Session II: Identification of available resources
	11:30–12:30	Lunch
	12:30–1:30	Prayer for the spirit of discernment[15]
	2:00–4:30	Session III: Identification of the priorities regarding the perceived needs; setting goals/ objectives for the coming year
	5:00–6:00	Liturgical celebration

The results of the discernment process utilized during this retreat are communicated to all small home-based groups, all groups involved in ministry, and all organizations and associations in the parish. Each parish group is invited to participate in the discernment process in order to set goals and objectives for the coming year, to provide feedback to the parish leadership regarding perceived priorities, and to participate in a parish assembly meeting at which goals and objectives for the coming year are decided and a pastoral planning committee is elected.

Various means of communication are used to inform the parish regarding the evolving ecclesial vision and the goals and objectives that deepen communion and further collaboration; all are invited to be active in mission and ministry. In the fall, parishioners are encouraged to participate in a parish assembly meeting and are asked to elect a pastoral planning committee.[16]

The pastoral planning committee includes members of the pastoral team, whose responsibilities include providing resources to all engaged in ministry to fulfill the goals and objectives, educating the parish regarding current developments in collaborative ministry, and reviewing annually the goals and objectives and identifying the current perceived needs that are not being addressed.

All home-based parish groups, ministry groups, organizations, and associations begin implementing the goals and objectives determined by the extensive process of consultation, which deepens communion and promotes collaboration. Six months later, the planning committee reviews the progress made in realizing the common goals and objectives during a Pentecost retreat. The design of the meeting is similar to the parish leadership retreat:

Friday	7:00–9:30 p.m.	Session I: Review utilization of resources to further the goals/objectives
	9:30–11:00	Social interaction: Informal discussion with facilitator
Saturday	9:00–11:30	Session II: Identification of current developments in collaborative ministry
	11:30–12:30	Lunch
	12:30–2:00	Prayer for the spirit of discernment
	2:30–5:00	Session III: Identification of the priorities regarding new perceived needs; setting new goals/objectives
	5:30–6:30	Liturgical celebration

The results of the discernment process utilized during the Pentecost planning retreat are communicated to all small home-based groups, the various groups involved in ministry, and the associations in the parish. The entire parish is given an account of current progress in developing collaborative ministry. Parish groups, organizations, and associations receive a report from the planning committee and respond to the planning committee by providing feedback and evaluation.

The parish is informed of how the goals and objectives are being implemented, communion is growing, collaboration is spreading among all, and increasing numbers are active in mission and ministry. In the fall, all parishioners are encouraged to participate in a parish assembly meeting to classify current perceived needs in the parish, to identify the necessary skills for developing collaborative ministry among all, to survey formation programs and resources currently available, and to set new goals and objectives for the coming year.

This two-year strategy utilizing the workshop on "Developing Collaborative Ministry Within the Parish," enables all to participate in a process that deepens communion and fosters a community in which all are active in ministry. The cycle contained in the strategy on Developing Collaborative Ministry Within the Parish can be repeated annually: communicating to all the benefits of collaborative ministry, educating all regarding the goals and objectives, inviting new people to form small groups to implement the workshop, identifying perceived needs and available resources, and integrating new goals and objectives with current pastoral planning.

The planning committee are responsible for identifying and collating the experiences, attitudes, programs, and community structures that are promoting collaborative ministry, and ensuring that these signs of growth are communicated throughout the parish.

One pastoral planning committee went on retreat to discern how it would address a root problem in the parish: individualism. It decided that (1) the model of the parish is a communion of small faith-sharing communities, (2) the parish be educated regarding the purpose, nature, and function of faith-sharing communities, (3) twenty leaders be selected to participate in a six-week course of formation on group process skills and the dynamics of small faith-sharing groups, and (4) twenty small faith-sharing groups be initiated, resourced, and supervised. The six-month review with this pastoral planning committee showed that the twenty groups engaged in faith-sharing have effectively enhanced communion in the parish.

The Role of Ministries

Vast numbers of people currently are engaged in some form of specialization in ministry, e.g. renewal center staff, seminary formation team, diocesan staff engaged in developing human resources, social concerns, education, and liturgy. The reflective process utilized in the workshop provides a useful resource for ongoing formation for all engaged in specialized types of ministries. The workshop identifies particular skills needed by all to promote collaborative ministry, integrates new members in a team ministry, and creates communion among all. The goals of the workshop are best realized when all teams engaged in ministry implement the workshop with their own colleagues in ministry.

The issues that surfaced from implementing the workshop with ordained and lay ministers engaged in team ministry are the need for reconciling different ecclesiological visions, developing a spiritual-formation program, training in leadership skills and leadership styles that promote collaborative ministry, and formation in supervised ministry, principles of feedback, support groups, self-evaluation, and group evaluation.

The consultants employed by many communities to facilitate formation in ministry are frequently without regular commitments to a particular community. These consultants need to discover the ongoing challenges presented by the workshop, "Developing Collaborative Ministry Within the Parish." A process is needed to promote cross-fertilization between specialized ministry teams and parishes, which have implemented the workshop on developing collaborative ministry. The greater the number of specialized ministry teams to implement the workshop, the greater the development of collaborative ministry within the diocese.

A follow-up process to the workshop designed to address this need is a diocesan day conference for all engaged in ministry; such a conference would bring together a large diversity of professional ministers with many experienced lay ministers. This conference for all engaged in ministry would be designed to develop mutual respect among professional specialized ministers and experienced professional and lay ministers engaged in development, to explore the forces that hinder the development of collaborative ministry and the processes that promote collaborative ministry among all, to promote a sharing of the collaborative vision of all engaged in ministry, and to celebrate the ongoing development of communion.[17]

Summary

Collaborative ministry is seldom initiated within the context of a reflective process that integrates an understanding of the ecclesiological, spiritual, and interpersonal dimensions of collaboration with a pastoral plan of implementation. The workshop addresses this problem by integrating ecclesiological theory with theological reflection and pastoral development.

The workshop on "Developing Collaborative Ministry Within the Parish" is designed to enable participants (1) to understand the Vatican II and post-conciliar teachings regarding collaboration in ministry, (2) to develop an appreciation of a collaborative style of spirituality, (3) to explore the leadership styles that facilitate collaborative ministry, and (4) to integrate the above dimensions in a local mission statement and pastoral plan for collaborative action. The workshop utilizes a reflective process that is designed to promote collaboration between ordained and lay ministers, and to enable all to be more effective in mission. The workshop provides a useful model for developing strategic pastoral planning and invites all engaged in ministry, all in formation, and all considering active ministry to promote cooperation, deepen communion, and develop collaborative ministry within the local church.

Conclusion

The ecclesiology of communion promoted in Vatican II and post-conciliar documents demonstrates the vision of what we are called to be as church. The workshop on "Developing Collaborative Ministry Within the Parish" promotes the development of communion among all participants, enables all the baptized to grow in holiness, utilizes the gifts of all in building the kingdom of God, respects the dignity of all, and promotes the collaboration of all in ministry.

Christ gathers the baptized and calls us to build up the kingdom of God, instilling in the church an experience of collegiality and communion. The baptized need a spiritual foundation that promotes cooperation, sustains collaborative forms of ministry, and deepens communion. Christ's presence in the individual empowers each person to share responsibility for the mission of the church, fulfills the universal call to discipleship, and generates communion. The workshop provides a spiritual foundation that sustains collaborative ministry by (1) integrating prayer, ministry, and liturgical celebration with a developed consciousness of mission, (2) deepening the experience of communion within the church, (3) enabling all to collaborate more effectively in ministry, and (4) utilizing the skills of all in building up the kingdom.

Leadership involves exercising authority where the leader's first responsibility is promoting communion and equality among all.[18] The workshop enables participants (1) to explore the leadership styles that promote communion and foster co-responsibility for the mission of the church (the semi-mutual and mutual styles of leadership), (2) to identify the leadership styles that hinder the development of collaborative ministry (the classic, autocratic style, and the charismatic), (3) to explore the ecclesiological foundation that sustains various leadership styles, (4) to distinguish the root causes of conflict and confrontation, and (5) to enable participants to utilize an appropriate leadership style that deepens communion in a diversity of pastoral settings.

Developing a mission statement integrates the ecclesial vision of communion and the spiritual foundation that sustains communion with the leadership styles that promote communion and generate collaborative ministry among all. The workshop explores a process that engages all the baptized in developing or reviewing the mission statement and identifying and utilizing the gifts of all in ministry. This process integrates an ecclesiological foundation for collaborative ministry with theological reflection and pastoral praxis. The process utilized in the development or review of the mission statement is educational, involves small-group interaction, promotes cooperation, deepens communion, and increases collaboration.

Utilizing a collaborative process to develop a pastoral plan addresses spiritual, physical, psychological, and social needs. This process is educational and helps to integrate the ecclesiological, spiritual, and interpersonal dimensions of collaboration with a plan of action. The reflective process utilized in the workshop (1) increases the number of people involved in an extensive process of consultation and discernment in which perceived needs are identified, goals are specified, and objectives are implemented, (2) fosters collaboration among a wider group of ministers and creates communion among all, (3) promotes the responsibility of all the baptized for the mission of the church, and (4) respects the diversity of gifts of all, encourages their use, and holds all accountable for their development.[19]

Collaborative ministry calls all the baptized to a communal expression of their priestly, prophetic, and royal ministry (1 Pet 2:4–5, 9–10), to a use of their gifts in building up the ecclesial community, to mutual respect, and to participation in dialogue. The workshop is designed to develop/review the mission statement and evaluate the implementation of the pastoral plan that enables the church to be a community in which all are active in ministry and act as leaven in society.

The workshop on "Developing Collaborative Ministry Within the Parish" promotes and affirms the areas where collaboration is operative, identifies the domain, the components, and the attitudes that hinder the development of collaborative ministry, and enables all to take responsibility for addressing the areas of resistance to developing collaborative ministry. The workshop provides a model for sustaining pastors, associate pastors, pastoral associates, those engaged in specialized ministries, everyone in formation for ministry, and the entire baptized community, being more effective in fulfilling the call to mission and ministry, furthering ecclesial development, enhancing faith formation, improving interpersonal skills, and revitalizing the parish.

Reflection

1. The benefits from implementing the workshop are . . .

2. The risks I can see in implementing the workshop are . . .

3. The group that would gain most from implementing the workshop is . . .

Suggested Reading

1. Robert G. Duch, *Successful Leadership: Nurturing the Animated Parish.*
    Kansas City: Sheed and Ward, 1990.

2. Loughlan Sofield and Brenda Hermann, *Developing the Parish as a Community of Service.* The Jesuit Educational Center for Human Development, 1984.

3. Cyril R. Mill, *Activities for Trainers: Fifty Useful Designs.* San Diego: University Associates, 1980.

ENDNOTES

CHAPTER I

1. Austin Flannery, ed., *Vatican II: The Conciliar and Post Conciliar Documents* (Northport: Costello, 1988), L.G. 32, 33, pp. 389–391; C.D. 16, pp. 572–573; A.G. 2, p. 814.

2. The Canon Law Society Trust, *Code of Canon Law* (London: Collins, 1983), Canons 129, p. 20; 460–66, pp. 82–83; 511–14, pp. 92; 517, p. 93; 536, p. 97.

3. 1985 Extraordinary Synod, The Final Report, II, C, 1 and 6 quoted in Leonard Doohan, *Grass Roots Pastors,* p. 36.

4. Ibid., p. 40.

5. Ibid., p. 41.

6. Ibid., p. 43.

7. Ibid., p. 44.

8. James H. Provost ed., *The Church as Communion,* Permanent Seminar Studies, No. 1 (Washington, DC: Canon Law Society of America, 1984), p. 11.

9. Karl Rahner, *The Church and the Sacraments* (New York: Herder and Herder, 1961), pp. 83–84.

10. John Paul II, *Christifideles Laici* (Boston: St. Paul's, 1989), p. 46.

11. James H. Provost, *The Church as Communion,* p. 12.

12. *Communion* is being rediscovered as an alternative model for structuring the church: Jerome Hamer, *The Church Is a Communion* (London: Geoffrey Chapman, 1964), pp. 159–213.

13. Paul VI, Wednesday General Audience (June 8, 1966): *Insegnamenti* IV, 794, quoted in *Christifideles Laici,* pp. 46–47.

14. Austin Flannery ed., *Vatican Council II: The Conciliar and Post Conciliar Documents* (Northport: Costello, 1987), L.G. 9, pp. 359–60.

15. *Christifideles Laici,* p. 48.

16. Extraordinary Synod of Bishops, *Origins* 15/27 (19 Dec. 1985), p. 449.

17. Leonard Doohan, *The Lay Centered Church* (Minneapolis: Winston Press, 1984), pp. 19–20.

18. Herbert Vorgrimler, ed., *Commentary on the Documents of Vatican II,* Vol III, *Decree on the Apostolate of the Laity* (New York: Herder and Herder, 1969), p. 337.

19. *The Code of Canon Law,* Canons 517, 519, p. 93; 759, p. 140; 766, p. 141; 1248, p. 217.

20. Doohan, *Grass Roots Pastors,* p. 12.

21. Ibid., pp. 13–14.

22. Vorgrimler, *Commentary,* Vol III, p. 397.

23. Herbert Vorgrimler, ed., *Commentary on the Documents of Vatican II,* Vol I, *Dogmatic Constitution on the Church* (New York: Herder and Herder, 1969), p. 264.

24. Ibid., p. 268.

25. Doohan, *Grass Roots Pastors,* p. 36.

26. Archbishop Donat Chiasson, "The People Born of Baptism," *Origins* 17/21 (5 Nov. 1987), pp. 393–94.

27. Bishops' Committee on Priestly Life and Ministry, "A Shepherd's Care: Reflections on the Changing Role of Pastor" (Washington, DC: U.S. Catholic Conference 1987), 17–18 quoted in *Origins* 17/19 (22 Oct. 1987), pp. 342–43.

28. Archbishop Hayes, "On Associating All the Baptized with Future Synods," *Origins* 17/19 (22 Oct. 1987), p. 344.

29. Archbishop Rembert Weakland, "Removing Obstacles That Impede Women," *Origins* 17/19 (22 Oct. 1987), p. 345.

30. Ibid.

31. Ibid.

32. "Partners in Redemption: A Pastoral Response to Women's Concerns for Church and Society." First Draft (Washington, DC: Office of Publishing and Promotion Services U.S.C.C., 1988), pp. 79–80.

33. *Christifideles Laici,* pp. 92–93.

34. Synod of Bishops, "On the Vocation and Mission of the Lay Faithful in the Church and in the World" (Oct. 1987), *propositiones* 46 & 47 quoted in *Christifideles Laici,* p. 127.

35. Ibid., p. 46.

36. Ibid., p. 131.

37. Ibid., pp. 135–136.

38. Ibid., p. 144.

39. Paul F. Bradshaw, "Lay Ministry Theories," *Doctrine and Life* 37/9 (1987), p. 510.

40. Extraordinary Synod of Bishops, Rome 1985. *A Message to the People of God and the Final Report* (Washington, DC: USCC, 1986), pp. 17–18.

CHAPTER II

1. Chiara Lubich is founder and president of an international ecumenical movement called the *Focolare*. She is the author of numerous books focusing on communal spirituality. In 1987 she addressed the Synod on the Laity on "Spirituality and Movements in the Church." Cf. Chiara Lubich, *Unity: Our Adventure* (New York: New City, 1987).

2. Chiara Lubich, *When Did We See You, Lord?* (New York: New City, 1980), p. 17.

3. Ibid., p. 21.

4. Robert L. Kinast, *Vatican II: Act II, Living in God's World* (Collegeville: Liturgical Press, 1990), pp. 16–25.

5. *Christifideles Laici,* p. 127.

6. Lubich, *When,* p. 106.

7. Chiara Lubich, *Jesus in the Midst,* (New York: New City, 1976), p. 22.

8. Ibid., p. 27.

9. Ibid., p. 38.

10. Ibid.

11. Ibid., pp. 39–40.

12. Ibid., p. 44.

13. Ibid., pp. 59–60.

14. Austin Flannery, ed., *Vatican II: The Conciliar and Post Conciliar Documents* (Northport: Costello, 1988), pp. 351, 784–85, 460–61.

15. Chiara Lubich, *Unity and Jesus Forsaken* (New York: New City, 1984), p. 12.

16. Loughlan Sofield and Carroll Juliano, *Collaborative Ministry* (Notre Dame: Ave Maria, 1987), pp. 63–65.

17. Anthony De Mello provides a series of spiritual exercises for entering the contemplative state blending psychology, spiritual therapy, and practices of both eastern and western traditions in *Sandhana: A Way to God* (New York: Doubleday, 1978).

18. Karl Rahner, "The Concept of Mystery in Catholic Theology," in *More Recent Writings: Theological Investigations,* vol. IV (London: Darton, Longman and Todd, 1966), pp. 36–73.

19. Ibid., p. 46.

20. Karl Rahner provides an overview of God as being the incomprehensible mystery in *Encounters with Silence* (Westminster: Christian Classics, 1984).

21. Thomas Keating provides a summary of the centering prayer method in *Open Mind, Open Heart: The Contemplative Dimension of the Gospel* (New York: Amity House, 1986), pp. 109–15.

22. Wilkie Au provides an outline of the apophatic and kataphatic methods of prayer

in *By Way of the Heart: Toward a Holistic Christian Spirituality* (New York: Paulist Press, 1989), pp. 96–113.

23. John Dalrymple, *Letting Go in Love: Reflections on Spiritual Formation* (Wilmington: Michael Glazier, 1988), pp. 78–79.

24. Henri J. Nouwen, *Reaching Out* (London: Doubleday, 1975), pp. 156–57.

25. Robert L. Miller and Gerard P. Weber provide group activities designed to raise consciousness, identify patterns of behavior, and promote change using storytelling and scripture in *Touchstone: An Activity Book for Adult Learners* (Allen: Tabor Publishing, 1987).

26. The characteristics of soul-friending are presented by William McNamara in *Christian Mysticism: The Art of the Inner Way* (New York: Amity House, 1981), pp. 49–73. The subject is dealt with in depth by Kenneth Leech in *Soul Friend: The Practice of Christian Spirituality* (New York: Harper and Row, 1977).

27. Doohan, *Grass Roots Pastors,* pp. 78–86, 175–83.

28. Sofield and Juliano, *Collaborative Ministry,* p. 65.

29. Gerard Rosse holds that the abandoned Christ is the God for our times, and is the source and measure of Christian love, in *The Cry of Jesus on the Cross: A Biblical and Theological Study* (New York: Paulist Press, 1987), p. 125.

30. Au, *By Way of the Heart,* pp. 50–55.

31. Lubich, *A Call to Love: Spiritual Writings,* Vol. 1. Translated by Hugh Moran (New York: New City, 1989), p. 94. [hereafter, *Call*]

32. Ibid., p. 85.

33. Ibid., p. 88.

34. Ibid., p. 91.

35. Ibid., p. 92.

36. Ibid., p. 95.

37. Flannery, *Vatican Council II,* S.C. 51, p. 17.

38. Ibid., D.V. 21, p. 762.

39. Lubich, *Call,* p. 98.

40. Ibid., pp. 112–13.

41. Re-membering is a one year process for inactive Catholics similar in design to the R.C.I.A. which prepares people for reintegration into the faith community during Holy Week. Cf. "The Re-Membering Ministry" *Catholic Evangelization* (May/June 1988), pp. 22–25.

42. The word *Focolare* means hearth or fire. This movement is ecumenical, exists in all five continents, and has over twelve million participants. Its founder Chiara Lubich received the Templeton prize "For Progress in Religion" in 1977, addressed the 1987 Synod on the Laity on "Spirituality and Movements in the Church," and in 1988 received the "Augsburg Festival of Peace Prize." Cf. "You Are Our Sister," *Living City* 28 (Jan. 1989), pp. 9–15.

43. Printed in sixty-nine languages, the "Word of Life" consists of a brief commentary by Chiara Lubich on a phrase of scripture taken from the Sunday lectionary, and communicated simultaneously to all countries in which *Focolare* exists. More than 3.3 million copies are regularly distributed, Groups meet to share their experiences of how they have lived the "Word of Life." Cf. Chiara Lubich, *Unity: Our Adventure* (New York: New City, 1987), pp. 64–67.

44. Flannery, *Vatican Council II,* S.C. 10, p. 6.

45. Lubich, *Call,* p. 128.

46. Ibid., p. 129.

47. Ibid.

48. Ibid., p. 130.

49. Thomas Richstatter explores this development in *Alternative Futures For Worship,* vol. III, *The Eucharist,* edited by Bernard J. Lee (Collegeville: Liturgical Press, 1987), pp. 120–21.

50. Flannery, *Vatican Council II,* S.C. 16–17, 47–48, pp. 8, 16–17.

51. Lubich, *Call,* p. 142.

52. Ibid., p. 140.

53. *Alternative Futures For Worship,* Vol. III, *The Eucharist,* p. 73.

54. Lubich, *Call,* p. 150.

55. Ibid., p. 153.

56. Karl Rahner, *Meditations on the Sacraments* (New York: Seabury Press, 1977), p. 39.

57. Flannery, *Vatican Council II,* A.A. 4, pp. 769–72.

58. Au, *By Way of the Heart,* p. 18.

59. Thomas Richstatter outlines how "the individual members of the assembly are so conjoined to the risen Lord that he and they are Christ now" in Bernard J. Lee, ed., *Alternative Futures for the Eucharist,* pp. 127–28.

60. Participation and Corresponsibility in the Church, Extraordinary Synod of Bishops, Rome 1985, "A Message to the People of God," *Origins* 15/27 (19 Dec. 1985), pp. 484–85.

CHAPTER III

1. James A. Coriden, "Options for the Organization of Ministry," *The Jurist* 40 (1981), pp. 484–86.

2. William Bausch, *Ministry: Traditions, Tensions, and Transitions* (Mystic: Twenty Third Publications, 1988), 122–23.

3. Ibid., p. 124.

4. Ibid., p. 123.

5. Ibid., pp. 124–25.

6. Ibid., p. 125.

7. Ibid., p. 127.

8. Fran Ferder and John Heagle, *Partnership: Women and Men in Ministry* (Notre Dame: Ave Maria Press, 1989), pp. 126–27.

9. A typical pastoral team is made up of the pastor, associate, deacon, liturgist, youth minister, minister of religious education, minister for adult education, minister for social concerns, parish sister, and administrator.

10. Doohan, *Grass Roots Pastors,* p. 71.

11. Ibid., pp. 72–73.

12. Bernard Swain, *Liberating Leadership: Practical Styles for Pastoral Ministry* (San Francisco: Harper and Row, 1986), pp. 67–69. [hereafter, *Liberating*]

13. Ibid., pp. 70–72.

14. Ibid., pp. 72–73.

15. Ibid., pp. 74–76.

16. Ibid., pp. 77–78.

17. Ibid., pp. 79–80.

18. Ibid., pp. 82–83.

19. Ibid., pp. 83–87.

20. Ibid., pp. 87–88.

21. Ibid., pp. 89–90.

22. Ibid., pp. 93–94.

23. Ibid., p. 95.

24. Ibid., p. 96.

25. Ibid., pp. 99–100.

26. Ibid., pp. 102–03.

27. Ibid., p. 104.

28. Ibid., pp. 113–14.

29. Ibid., pp. 116–17.

30. Ibid., pp. 117–19.

31. A team-building activity that develops giving and receiving feedback on work-related and personal-growth goals and promoting team support on one another's goals is available in Pfeiffer's *1985 Developing,* pp. 87–89.

32. Swain, *Liberating,* pp. 120–21.

33. The pastor sets the tone of the parish. When he uses a "pluralistic" form of leadership, all the available resources in the community are utilized to ensure that everyone has a ministry. Jim Castelli and Joseph Gremillion, *The Emerging Parish* (San Francisco: Harper and Row, 1987), p. 113. [hereafter, *Emerging*]

34. Bishop William Hughes, "Not Lords, But Servants," *Origins* 15/29 (2 Jan. 1986), p. 481.

35. Ibid., p. 482.

36. A comprehensive character inventory that fosters group communication, identi-
fies perceived needs of working teams, and promotes team development is provided by
Steven L. Phillips and Robert L. Elledge in *The Team-Building Source Book* (San Diego:
University Associates, 1989), pp. 22–36.

37. Marrianne Corey and Gerald Corey, *Groups: Process and Practice* (Monterey:
Brooks/Cole Publishing Co., 1987), p. 56. [hereafter *Groups*]

38. An interesting conflict simulation is available in J. William Pfeiffer, *The 1987
Annual: Developing Human Resources* (San Diego: University Associates, 1987),
pp. 79–86.

39. Corey, *Groups,* p. 144.

40. Doohan, *Grass Roots,* p. 168.

41. Associate pastors are the most likely group of leaders to report conflict. They
think that it exists mostly between parish staff and pastoral council, pastor and staff, or
pastor and pastoral council. Castelli and Gremillion, *Emerging,* p. 107.

42. Corey, *Groups,* pp. 145–47.

43. An exercise that develops participants' understanding of how to give and receive
feedback, the impact of receiving feedback, and how feedback helps an individual or group
to improve their effectiveness is given in Pfeiffer's *1989 Developing,* pp. 9–12.

44. Swain, *Liberating,* pp. 105–07.

45. Ibid., pp. 108–09.

46. The principles of giving and receiving feedback from peers, supervisors, and
subordinates are outlined in Pfeiffer's *1989 Developing,* pp. 13–16.

47. Swain, *Liberating,* pp. 109–111.

CHAPTER IV

1. Loughlan Sofield and Brenda Hermann, *Developing the Parish as a Community of
Service* (The Jesuit Educational Center for Human Development, 1984), p. 18.

2. Pertinent data concerning the local community and how to integrate this with the
parish data are outlined in William C. Harms, *Who Are We, and Where Are We Going? A
Guide for Parish Planning* (New York: Sadlier, 1981), pp. 36–40.

3. Answers are needed to the following questions: What does each member of the
parish need to grow to the fullness of his or her Christian vocation? What will help the
parish to grow closer to the ideal of being a community of service? What gifts and talents
exist in our parish that can be utilized in ministry? What community issues need to be
addressed by our parish? Sofield, *Developing,* pp. 19–20.

4. The relevant documents are: *Sacrosanctum Concilium, Lumen Gentium, Unitatis
Redintegratio, Apostolicam Actuositatem, Ad Gentes,* and *Gaudium et Spes.* Austin Flan-

nery, ed., *Vatican Council II* (Northport: Costello Publishing, 1988), pp. 1–100, 452–501, 766–98, 813–63, 903–1001.

5. Sofield, *Developing,* pp. 21–22, 82–86.

6. Ibid., p. 23.

7. Setting goals fosters the sharing of responsibility in the church. The principles involved in setting, writing and testing the quality of goals are outlined in Harms, *Who Are We?* pp. 53–60.

8. Sofield, *Developing,* pp. 23–24, 94–97.

9. The facilitator can be any one of the following: the pastor, one of the two consultants employed in the formation of the group leaders, a member of the parish team, or a member of the pastoral council.

10. Sofield, *Developing,* pp. 98–100.

11. Ibid., p. 27.

12. The theologian or canon lawyer employed to educate the small group leaders about the Vatican II documents provides the necessary materials/resources to be used for reflection.

13. Sofield, *Developing,* p. 28.

14. Means for promoting spiritual growth include: gospel-sharing, group liturgy, shared faith experience, shared prayer, group discernment, and group mutual correction. Doohan, *Grass Roots Pastors,* pp. 78–84.

15. All parish groups are engaged in praying for the renewal committee while they discern an appropriate theme for the parish spiritual formation week.

16. The facilitator can be the pastor, associate, or any member of the pastoral team or pastoral council.

17. The search committee is made up of the pastor or associate, the facilitator of the renewal committee, the chairperson of the pastoral council, and a member from the parish personnel board.

18. Sofield, *Developing,* pp. 29–30.

19. Ibid., p. 31.

20. *Christifideles Laici,* p. 48.

21. The communications' coordinator can be selected from any of the current ministers in the parish who have the necessary skill and pastoral competence to address the need for improving communication within the parish.

22. "As Christ was anointed Priest, Prophet, and King, so may you live always as a member of his body, sharing everlasting life." The Rite of Baptism, no. 98, in *The Rites of the Catholic Church* (New York: Pueblo Publishing Co., 1976), p. 223.

CHAPTER V

1. Harms, *Who Are We?* pp. 53–66.

2. Members of the planning committee are required to commit themselves to working seventy hours per year: thirty hours will be given to an overnight planning retreat; the remaining forty hours will be used in regular meetings and training sessions.

3. Paul M. Deitterich, *Practical Guide to Church Planning: A Church Vitalization Resource* (Chicago: The Center for Parish Development, 1981), pp. 27–30. [hereafter *Practical Guide*]

4. Deitterich, *Practical Guide,* pp. 11–15.

5. Ibid., p. 28.

6. Structured experiences that aid the planning team and church leaders in making strategic decisions, combined with the appropriate tactical decisions, are provided by Dietterich, in *Practical Guide,* pp. 151–61.

7. J. William Pfeiffer, Leonard D. Goodstein and Timothy M. Nolan, *Understanding Applied Strategic Planning: A Manager's Guide* (San Diego: University Associates Inc., 1985), pp. 2–9.

8. Developing a parish plan of action, integrating diverse ministries, and planning a calendar is described in Harms, *Who Are We?* pp. 67–74.

9. A planning sheet that focuses on the development of a mission statement and pastoral plan is available in Sofield, *Developing,* 94–97.

10. A calendar outlining one year's parish activities is given in Harms, *Who Are We?* p. 74.

11. *The Parish Self-Study Guide,* based on the Bishops' Vision Statement, *The Parish: A People, A Mission, A Structure,* provides resources for evaluating staff leadership (Washington, DC: NCCB, 1980), pp. 64–79.

12. An evaluation and recycling process is outlined in Harms, *Who Are We?* pp. 76–80.

13. Sofield, *Developing,* pp. 49–52.

14. A self-evaluation questionnaire focusing on the ability to work with others is available in Doohan, *Grass Roots Pastors,* pp. 87–90.

15. Deitterich provides a comprehensive guide for evaluating the process of strategic planning in *Practical Guide,* pp. 301–28.

16. Doohan provides questionnaires that help the parish evaluate its ministers in *Grass Roots Pastors,* pp. 90–98.

17. Harms provides a workbook for pastoral planning in *Who Are We?* pp. 81–112.

18. Sofield, *Developing,* pp. 52–55, 144.

19. Deitterich, *Practical Guide,* pp. 272–78.

CHAPTER VI

1. The process is designed to utilize the skills of two facilitators. The co-facilitators require a theological foundation and skills in group process, counseling, faith-sharing, conflict management and pastoral planning. Mutuality and co-responsibility in ministry is manifested when the co-facilitators represent male, female, lay, and ordained ministers. Many professional and full-time pastoral ministers possess the basic skills to become co-facilitators of the workshop. Cf. Archdiocese of Chicago, *Coordinating Parish Ministries* (Chicago: Department of Personnel Services, 1987), pp. 25–30.

2. The facilitators present a consent form outlining the reflective process utilized in the workshop, which includes information on confidentiality, scheduling, benefits, risks, and cost. Appendix B.

3. A group's commitment to formation is evident from the proportion of the annual budget allocated to human resource training and development. The higher the cost of the workshop, the greater the commitment of the group to active preparation and participation.

4. An appropriate time is needed between sessions to integrate theory, reflection, and praxis: one session each month has proved to be effective.

5. The reflection questions enable the participants to integrate their pastoral praxis with an ecclesiological, spiritual, and interpersonal foundation for collaborative ministry. Appendix D.

6. A package that focuses on the evaluation process is available from Dr. J. Michael McMahon, 1427 West Braddock Road, Alexandria, VA 22302.

7. A detailed account of the evaluation results is available from Dr. J. Michael McMahon, 1427 West Braddock Road, Alexandria, VA 22302.

8. One facilitator is responsible for delivering the presentation in Sessions I, III, and V, and also for facilitating the group process in Sessions II and IV. The other facilitator is accountable for delivering the presentation in Sessions II and IV, and for facilitating the group process in Sessions I, III, and V.

9. Information on previous groups that implemented the workshop is available from Dr. J. Michael McMahon, 1427 West Braddock Road, Alexandria, VA 22302.

10. An outline of the benefits, risks, and issues raised by other groups' experience of the workshop is available from Dr. J. Michael McMahon, 1427 West Braddock Road, Alexandria, VA 22302.

11. Possible schedules include one weekly session during Lent or Advent, a three-day residential experience, three full days one week apart, or two evenings including overnights and all day sessions, one month apart.

12. The group meeting following the completion of the workshop focuses on identifying an area of resistance to collaborative ministry, naming the skills that need to be

developed to further collaborative ministry, and establishing goals and objectives that address these perceived needs in the coming year.

13. This schedule is flexible and can be adapted by individual parishes to meet their particular needs.

14. The consultant is required to possess an awareness of current developments in collaborative ministry and the skills necessary for effective pastoral planning.

15. A possible format for the prayer is: naming the perceived needs expressed by the community (20 minutes), silent refection (20 minutes), and public intercession for the expressed needs of the community (20 minutes).

16. A comprehensive process for parish-based planning is *Companions on the Journey* (Saginaw: Diocesan Planning Coordinating Committee, 1992).

17. The diocesan assembly for all ministers could begin on Friday evening at 7:00 p.m. It may include three keynote presentations, a variety of workshops, an opportunity for small group sharing, an open forum, and a liturgical celebration, and conclude with dinner at 7:00 p.m. on Saturday.

18. Robert K. Greenleaf, *Servant Leadership* (New York: Paulist Press, 1977), p. 241.

19. The workshop utilizes adult learning principles as outlined in Robert G. Duch, *Sucessful Parish Leadership: Nurturing the Animated Parish* (Kansas City: Sheed and Ward, 1990), pp. 203–06.

APPENDIX A

Developing Collaborative Ministry Within the Parish

I Purpose:

—**To enable** all ordained and lay ministers engaged in ministry to work together more effectively.

—**To support and encourage** the sharing of our common faith and common vision of church.

—**To facilitate** the development of each individual's ministry.

II Aim:

—**The clarification** of the strengths and effectiveness of ordained and lay ministers engaged in collaborative forms of ministry.

—**The identification** of areas requiring further development of collaborative ministry.

—**The integration** of the ecclesiological, spiritual, and interpersonal components that facilitate collaborative ministry with a pastoral plan of action.

III Commitment:

—**The sessions** consist of a series of two-and-a-half-hour workshops that take place in either the morning, afternoon, or evening.
—**Five consecutive weekly meetings, three two day meetings,** or **a weekend.**
—**Timing:** mutually decided upon by facilitator(s) and the participants.
—**Attendance required** by all participants at each of the five sessions.

IV The Structure:

The content is presented utilizing a **didactic** methodology. The design employs a **collaborative** model. **Reading** pertinent to the various sessions is suggested.

Session I: An **Ecclesiological** Foundation for Collaborative Ministry.

Session II: A **Spiritual** Foundation for Collaborative Ministry.

Session III: The **Relational Dynamics** That Facilitate Collaborative Ministry.

Session IV: The **Integration** of the **Ecclesiological, Spiritual,** and **Relational** Components with the Parish Mission Statement.

Session V: The **Evaluation/Development** of a Parish Pastoral Plan.

V Facilitator(s):

The facilitators provide an overview of their professional experience and competence.

VI Participant's Evaluation

The following evaluations were made by ordained and lay ministers who participated in the workshop.

The thing I liked best about the workshop was:
—the opportunity for our staff to dialogue about our leadership style and our vision of ministry;
—I was able to share faith (not just programs) with other staff members;
—I could see and feel God's presence among us, especially during the reflection and small-group sharing.

The major benefit I received from the workshop was:
—a clearer understanding of why I am sometimes unable to make myself understood, an awareness that I have been formed as a minister through the workshop, and the knowledge that I'll have a much harder time actually collaborating;
—receiving resources and not having responsibility (for once) of being a resource to others;
—a stronger vision of leadership styles: strengths and weaknesses; a challenge to develop more consciously pastoral planning, evaluation, support, and feedback.

APPENDIX B

Establishing a Contract: Consent Form

DEVELOPING COLLABORATIVE MINISTRY WITHIN THE PARISH

Purpose of the Workshop

The purpose of this workshop is to implement a reflective process that will help individual ordained and lay ministers:

(1) to understand the Vatican II teachings and post-conciliar teachings regarding communion and collaboration;
(2) to develop an appreciation of a collaborative style of spirituality;
(3) to explore the interpersonal skills and leadership styles that facilitate collaborative ministry;
(4) to integrate the above dimensions in a local parish mission statement and pastoral plan for collaborative action.

Procedures To Be Followed

The workshop on "Developing Collaborative Ministry Within the Parish" will consist of five two-and-a-half-hour sessions that seek to integrate theory, reflection, and praxis.

(1) *Theory:* Participants will be presented with: an ecclesiology of communion that facilitates collaborative ministry; a model of spirituality that respects the equal dignity of all, empowers the recognition of Christ in all, and promotes communion through living out the word of God; the interpersonal skills and leadership styles that sustain communion and develop collaborative ministry within the parish team; a discernment process whereby the above can be integrated into a pastoral plan for action in their parish.

(2) *Reflection:* Participants will prepare for each presentation with assigned reading and by keeping a journal. Each session will begin with a presentation (30 mins.). Participants then will be given time to answer two set questions (20 mins.). Small-group sharing based on these answers (30 mins.) will be followed by large-group sharing (40 mins.), and finally the session will be concluded by the facilitator(s) (30 mins.).

(3) *Praxis:* Participants will develop a parish mission statement and a pastoral plan based upon an ecclesiology of communion that facilitates collaborative ministry, a spirituality that promotes communion through living out the word of God, and the interpersonal skills and leadership styles that sustain communion and empower collaborative ministry within the parish team.

Each of the five sessions of the workshop lasts two-and-a-half hours and will deal with the following topics:

Session I	The ecclesiology of communion presented in Vatican II, the 1985 Extraordinary Synod of Bishops, and John Paul II's *Christifideles Laici:* a foundation for collaborative ministry.
II	A model of spirituality that facilitates communion and empowers collaborative ministry.
III	The leadership styles that promote communion and foster collaborative ministry: focus on training, evaluation, feedback, and supervision.
IV	The ecclesiological, spiritual, and interpersonal concepts that promote communion: the integration of these concepts with the parish vision and mission statement facilitates collaborative ministry.

V   The integration of the above concepts with a collaborative model used to promote communion and develop a pastoral plan for the particular parish.

Participants will complete a written evaluation questionnaire "before the five sessions" to determine: (1) their ecclesiological perception, (2) their spiritual heritage, (3) their competence in group process and skills, and (4) their experience in pastoral planning. Participants will complete the same written evaluation questionnaire at the end of the fifth session, to ascertain any change in the participants' perception regarding the four categories listed above. The fifth session will conclude with a third written evaluation questionnaire which will be used for discussion with the facilitator(s) in order to ascertain their effectiveness as educators, ministers, and facilitators in the collaborative process.

Benefits

The workshop will attempt to deepen participants' understanding of Vatican II's teaching and post-conciliar teaching regarding collaboration, to develop their appreciation of a collaborative style of spirituality, to empower them to be more effective leaders, and to integrate their ministerial service with a pastoral plan for action.

Risks

The workshop may highlight the need for ongoing training, formation, supervision, and evaluation in the following areas:

Ecclesiological study;

Spiritual development and enrichment;

Leadership styles;

Pastoral planning and implementation.

Cost

Each parish participating in the workshop will be charged $\$$____ for each of the five two-and-a-half-hour sessions. The total charge of $\$$____ will be paid to the facilitator(s) upon the completion of the fifth and final session.

Consent

I volunteer to participate in the above workshop and have received a signed copy of this consent form. I may discontinue my participation in the workshop at any time. I understand that any information about me obtained as a result of my participation in this workshop will be kept as confidential as possible. I have had an opportunity to ask questions about the workshop, and any questions regarding confidentiality have been answered to my satisfaction.

_____   _____

Participants's Signature   Facilitator's Signature

    Date _____   _____

                                             Facilitator's Signature

                                              Date _____

APPENDIX C

Schedules

Schedule I

Tuesday:	SESSION I	3:00–5:30
	Dinner	5:45–6:30
	SESSION II	7:00–9:30
	Cheese/Wine	9:30–10:30
Wednesday:	Breakfast	8:00–8:45
	Morning Prayer	9:00–9:30
	SESSION III	9:30–12:00
	Lunch	12:30–1:30
	SESSION IV	2:00–4:30
	Eucharist	5:00–5:45
	Dinner	5:45–6:30
	Individual Consultation	7:00–9:00
Thursday:	Breakfast	8:00–8:45
	Morning Prayer	9:00–9:30
	SESSION V	9:30–12:00
	Lunch	12:30–1:30
	Individual Consultation	1:30–2:30
	EVALUATION	2:30–3:30

Schedule II

Week I	*Saturday:*	SESSION I	1:00–3:30
		Individual	
		Consultation	3:30–4:30
Week II	*Sunday:*	SESSION II	5:30–8:00
Week III	*Monday:*	Individual	
		Consultation	6:00–7:30
		SESSION III	7:30–10:00
Week IV	*Sunday:*	SESSION IV	7:30–10:00
Week V	*Saturday:*	Individual	
		Consultation	9:00–10:00
		SESSION V	10:00–12:30
		EVALUATION	1:00–2:00

Schedule III

	Thursday:	SESSION I	3:00–5:30
		Dinner	6:00–7:00
		Individual	
		Consultation	7:00–8:30
	Friday:	SESSION II	9:30–12:00
		Lunch	12:30–1:30
		SESSION III	2:00–4:30
		Dinner	6:00–7:00
		Individual	
		Consultation	7:00–8:30
	Saturday:	SESSION IV	9:30–12:00
		Lunch	12:30–1:30
	Saturday:	SESSION V	10:00–12:30
	(one week later)	EVALUATION	1:00–2:00

Schedule IV

| | *Monday:* | SESSION I | 9:00–11:30 |
| | | Lunch | 11:30–12:30 |

	SESSION II	12:30–3:00
	Individual	
	Consultation	3:00–4:30
Monday:	SESSION III	9:00–11:30
(one week later)	Lunch	11:30–12:30
	SESSION IV	12:30–3:00
	Individual	
	Consultation	3:00–4:30
Monday:	SESSION V	9:00–11:30
(one week later)	Lunch	11:30–12:30
	EVALUATION	1:00–2:00

Schedule V

	Unit I	
Friday (pm)	SESSION I	7:00–9:30
Informal discussion		
with facilitator(s)		9:30–11:00
Saturday	SESSION II	9:30–11:30
	Lunch	11:30–12:30
Individual consultation		
with facilitator(s)		12:30–2:30
	SESSION III	2:30–5:00
Liturgical celebration		5:30–6:30
	Unit II	
(One month later)	SESSION IV	7:30–9:00
Friday (pm)		
Informal discussion		
with facilitator(s)		9:30–11:00
Saturday	SESSION V	9:30–11:00
	Lunch	11:30–12:30
Individual consultation		
with facilitator(s)		12:30–2:00
	EVALUATION	2:00–3:00
Liturgical celebration		3:00–4:00

APPENDIX D

Suggested Reading and Reflection Questions

Session I.   The ecclesiology of communion presented in Vatican II, the 1985 Synod of Bishops, and John Paul II's *Christifideles Laici:* a foundation for collaborative ministry. Read: Michael A. Fahey, "Ecclesial Community as Communion," *The Church as Communion,* James H. Provost ed. (Washington, DC: Canon Law Society of America Permanent Seminar Studies 1, 1984), pp. 4–23.

Reflection:

(1)   I experienced intense communion with the risen Lord when

_____

_____

(2)   I felt profound communion with others during

_____

_____

Session II.   A model of spirituality that facilitates communion and empowers collaborative ministry. Read: Chiara Lubich, *From Scripture to Life* (New York: New City Press, 1991).

Wilkie Au. *By Way of the Heart: Toward a Holistic Christian Spirituality* (Mahwah: Paulist Press, 1989), pp. 85–113.

Leonard Doohan. *Grass Roots Pastors: A Handbook For Career Lay Ministers* (San Francisco: Harper and Row, 1989), pp. 78–84.

Reflection:

(1) A phrase of scripture that I have lived and made incarnate in my life and that is significant for me is

_____

_____

(2) A way of praying that I find most useful is

_____

_____

(3) A method of faith-sharing that appeals to me is

_____

Session III. The leadership styles that promote communion and foster collaborative ministry focus on training, evaluation, feedback and supervision. Read: Leonard Doohan, *Grass Roots Pastors,* pp. 46–60, 73–77, 84–87, 168–71.

Reflection:

(1) The style of leadership I use most often in my ministry is

_____

(2) A leadership style I experienced as being inappropriate to a particular situation in ministry was manifested when

_____

_____

Session IV. The ecclesiological, spiritual, and interpersonal concepts that promote communion: the integration of these concepts with the parish mission statement facilitates collaborative ministry.

Read: Loughlan Sofield and Brenda Hermann, *Developing the Parish As a Community of Service* (The Jesuit Educational Center for Human Development, 1984), pp. 1–57.

Reflection:
  (1) How many parishioners participated in the process used to develop our mission statement, and what percentage are conscious of the content, and are actively involved in living out our mission?
  (2) Greater co-responsibility for the mission of our community can be generated by _____

  _____

Session V. The integration of the above concepts with a collaborative model used to promote communion and develop a pastoral plan for the parish. Read: Archdiocese of Milwaukee, *Walking Together: Collaborating for the Future—Parish Planning Resource Booklet* (Milwaukee: Steering Committee for Parish Planning, 1989), pp. 8–29, 37–40.

Reflection:
  (1) What excites me about our common call to create the future church together is

  _____

  _____

  (2) The greatest obstacle to creating a renewed experience of church is

  _____

  _____

  (3) To prepare collaboratively for mission and ministry we need

  _____

  _____

APPENDIX E

Evaluation Questionnaires

INITIAL WORKSHOP QUESTIONNAIRE

Please take a few minutes to fill out this questionnaire.

Name _____

Address _____

_____

Phone _____ (Day) _____ (Evening)

Parish _____

How many years have you been involved in full-time ministry? _____

What is your specific ministry?

_____

_____

What did your training for ministry consist of?

_____

_____

How long have you been a member of this pastoral team? _____

During the workshop we will be exploring our understanding of the church, our spiritual heritage, the leadership styles that facilitate collaboration in ministry, and the importance of pastoral planning. It will be helpful to reflect on our current attitudes to these issues before we begin the workshop.

**Please respond to the following statements
by circling the appropriate number.**

1	2	3	4	5
strongly disagree	disagree	uncertain	agree	strongly agree

(1)   My vision of the church determines how I understand ministry.

                            1   2   3   4   5

(2)   Because Christ is present in all, we are all equal partners in ministry.

                            1   2   3   4   5

(3)   The leadership style adopted by our pastoral team determines our degree of collaboration.

                            1   2   3   4   5

(4)   Partnership in ministry requires a greater depth of self-awareness and a willingness to cooperate.

                            1   2   3   4   5

(5)   My spirituality focuses on

       (number 1–5 in order of importance; 5 = highest)

       _____ Caring for the environment
       _____ Faith in action
       _____ Being holistic
       _____ Communion with God and others
       _____ Personal development

(6) The church is the people of God in which communion ought to be *the* central experience.

1   2   3   4   5

(7) Christ can be present even when we experience tension and conflict within the pastoral team.

1   2   3   4   5

(8) I understand the church to be

(number 1–5 in order of importance; 5 = highest)

_____ Mission
_____ Institution
_____ Communion
_____ Sacrament
_____ Community of Disciples

(9) Each member of the pastoral team should be trained in leadership skills that facilitate cooperation and co-responsibility.

1   2   3   4   5

(10) To participate effectively in pastoral planning I need

_____

_____

(11) The church needs to be experienced as communion in order to fulfill its mission in the world.

1   2   3   4   5

(12) Supervision, feedback, and evaluation are crucial for collaborative ministry.

1   2   3   4   5

(13) Our type of spirituality increases our collaboration in ministry.

1   2   3   4   5

(14) Tension, criticism, and negativity hinder the development of collaborative ministry.

1   2   3   4   5

(15) My strongest experience of the mission of the church was

_____

_____

_____

(16) Living the word of God is necessary for collaborative ministry.

1   2   3   4   5

(17) Ministry in our parish is a corporate undertaking in which all the baptized are equally responsible.

1   2   3   4   5

(18) What I need most to develop my vision of the church is

_____

_____

_____

(19) Shared responsibility for ministry between ordained and lay ministers in this parish is

              _____ the exception

              _____ normative

(number 1–5 according to your   _____ rare

lived experience; 5 = highest)   _____ a growing reality

              _____ a dream

(20) The greater the degree of collaboration among the members of the pastoral team, the more effectively we fulfill our mission.

1   2   3   4   5

(21)   The parish leadership could help me to grow spiritually by

_____

_____

_____

(22)   Collaborative ministry requires commitment to training and supervision in ministry.

                        1   2   3   4   5

(23)   Christ's presence always is felt within our pastoral team.

                        1   2   3   4   5

(24)   Conflict and confrontation need to be addressed in order to facilitate collaborative ministry.

                        1   2   3   4   5

(25)   One instance of mutual respect I experienced between ordained and lay ministers was

_____

_____

_____

(26)   All the baptized are equally responsible for this parish's ministry.

                        1   2   3   4   5

(27)   My training/experience in pastoral planning is

                                    _____   limited
       (number 1–5 in order of   _____   comprehensive
       importance; 5 = highest)   _____   adequate
                                    _____   non-existent
                                    _____   inadequate

(28)   What makes collaborative ministry difficult in our present pastoral set-
        ting is

        _____

        _____

(29)   We need to develop/reevaluate our parish's mission statement.

                        1   2   3   4   5

(30)   Based on my own experience of ministry in the church, the model that
        best describes my vision of collaborative ministry is

        _____

        _____

        _____

        _____

**A booklet explaining the evaluation process is available from Dr. John
Harrington, Blessed Sacrament Catholic Community, 1427 West Braddock
Road, Alexandria, VA 22302.**

CONCLUDING WORKSHOP QUESTIONNAIRE

Name _____

Parish _____

During this workshop we have examined our understanding of the church, our spiritual heritage, the interpersonal skills and leadership styles that facilitate collaboration in ministry, and the importance of pastoral planning. Before the workshop, you responded to each of the following statements by indicating your level of agreement or disagreement. Now you are asked to indicate the extent to which your attitude toward each statement may have changed by comparing your response to the initial workshop questionnaire with this questionnaire.

Please respond to each statement with a number between 0 and 100. A response of 50 indicates that you have the same level of agreement or disagreement with each statement. If you agree more strongly with a particular statement, please circle a number between 60 and 100. Lower numbers indicate slightly more agreement and higher numbers indicate much stronger agreement. If you disagree more strongly with a particular statement, please circle a number between 0 and 40. Higher numbers indicate slightly less disagreement, and lower numbers indicate much stronger disagreement.

             0   10   20   30   40   50   60   70   80   90   100

strongly   same   strongly
disagree   agree

(1)   My ecclesial vision determines how I understand ministry.

             0   10   20   30   40   50   60   70   80   90   100

(2)   Because Christ is present in all, we are all equal partners in ministry.

             0   10   20   30   40   50   60   70   80   90   100

(3)   The leadership style adopted by our pastoral team determines our degree of collaboration.

             0   10   20   30   40   50   60   70   80   90   100

(4)   Partnership in ministry requires a greater depth of self-awareness and a
       willingness to cooperate.

       0   10   20   30   40   50   60   70   80   90   100

(5)   My spirituality focuses on   _____   Caring for the
                                                        environment
       i   (number 1–5 in order of   _____   Faith in action
           importance; 5 = highest)   _____   Being holistic
                                            _____   communion with God
                                                        and others
       ii (60–100 = more convinced)   _____   personal
           (0–40 = less convinced)   development

       0   10   20   30   40   50   60   70   80   90   100

(6)   The church is the people of God in which communion ought to be *the*
       central experience.

       0   10   20   30   40   50   60   70   80   90   100

(7)   Christ can be present even when we experience tension and conflict
       within the pastoral team.

       0   10   20   30   40   50   60   70   80   90   100

(8)   I understand the church to be
                                            _____   Mission
       i   (number 1–5 in order of   _____   Institution
           importance; 5 = highest)   _____   Communion
                                            _____   Sacrament
       ii (60–100 = more convinced)   _____   Community of
           (0–40 = less convinced)   Disciples

       0   10   20   30   40   50   60   70   80   90   100

(9)   Each member of the pastoral team should be trained in leadership skills
       that facilitate cooperation and co-responsibility.

       0   10   20   30   40   50   60   70   80   90   100

(10)   To participate effectively in pastoral planning I need

_____

_____

    0 10 20 30 40 50 60 70 80 90 100

(11)   The church needs to be experienced as communion in order to fulfill its mission in the world.

    0 10 20 30 40 50 60 70 80 90 100

(12)   Supervision, feedback, and evaluation are crucial for collaborative ministry.

    0 10 20 30 40 50 60 70 80 90 100

(13)   Our type of spirituality increases our collaboration in ministry.

    0 10 20 30 40 50 60 70 80 90 100

(14)   Tension, criticism, and negativity hinder the development of collaborative ministry.

    0 10 20 30 40 50 60 70 80 90 100

(15)   My strongest experience of the mission of the church was

_____

_____

_____

    0 10 20 30 40 50 60 70 80 90 100

(16)   Living the word of God is necessary for collaborative ministry.

    0 10 20 30 40 50 60 70 80 90 100

(17)   Ministry in our parish is a corporate undertaking in which all the baptized are equally responsible.

    0 10 20 30 40 50 60 70 80 90 100

(18)   What I need most to develop my vision of the church is

_____

_____

_____

0   10   20   30   40   50   60   70   80   90   100

(19)   Shared responsibility for ministry between ordained and lay ministers in this parish is

_____ the exception
_____ normative

i   (number 1–5 according to your   _____ rare
lived experience; 5 = highest)   _____ a growing reality
_____ a dream

ii   (60–100 = more convinced)
(0–40 = less convinced)

0   10   20   30   40   50   60   70   80   90   100

(20)   The greater the degree of collaboration among the members of the pastoral team, the more effectively we fulfill our mission.

0   10   20   30   40   50   60   70   80   90   100

(21)   The parish leadership could help me to grow spiritually by

_____

_____

0   10   20   30   40   50   60   70   80   90   100

(22)   Collaborative ministry requires commitment to training and supervision in ministry.

0   10   20   30   40   50   60   70   80   90   100

(23) Christ's presence always is felt within our pastoral team.

      0   10   20   30   40   50   60   70   80   90   100

(24) Conflict and confrontation need to be addressed in order to facilitate collaborative ministry.

      0   10   20   30   40   50   60   70   80   90   100

(25) One instance of mutual respect I experienced between ordained and lay ministers was

_____

_____

      0   10   20   30   40   50   60   70   80   90   100

(26) All the baptized are equally responsible for this parish's ministry.

      0   10   20   30   40   50   60   70   80   90   100

(27) My training/experience in pastoral planning is

                                  _____ limited

i (number 1–5 in order of   _____ comprehensive
   importance 5 = highest)   _____ adequate

                                  _____ non-existent

ii (60–100 = more convinced)   _____ inadequate
   (0–50 = less convinced)

      0   10   20   30   40   50   60   70   80   90   100

(28) What makes collaborative ministry difficult in our present pastoral setting is

_____

_____

      0   10   20   30   40   50   60   70   80   90   100

(29) We need to develop/reevaluate our parish's vision/mission statement.

      0   10   20   30   40   50   60   70   80   90   100

(30)   Based on my own experience of ministry in the church, the model that best describes my vision of collaborative ministry is

_____

_____

_____

       0   10   20   30   40   50   60   70   80   90   100

Please mail all the completed evaluation questionnaires for processing to Dr. John Harrington, Blessed Sacrament Catholic Community, 1427 West Braddock Road, Alexandria, VA 22302.

EVALUATION OF THE WORKSHOP AND THE FACILITATORS

Name: _____

During the workshop, the facilitators attempted to exercise their skills as educators, ministers and facilitators of collaborative ministry. How effectively did they exercise these skills during the workshop? Your response to the following questions will form the basis for discussion with the facilitators, to evaluate their effectiveness as educators, ministers and facilitators of collaborative ministry. Please respond to each of the following statements by circling the appropriate number.

1	2	3	4	5
strongly disagree	disagree	uncertain	agree	strongly agree

(1)   The workshop helped me to gain new insights.

             1   2   3   4   5

(2)   The workshop will make a difference in my ministry within the pastoral team.

             1   2   3   4   5

(3)   The workshop process was well designed.

             1   2   3   4   5

(4)   The workshop addressed real concerns of the participants.

             1   2   3   4   5

(5)   The facilitators took seriously the experience and input of the participants.

             1   2   3   4   5

(6)   The facilitators gave presentations that were clear and engaging.

             1   2   3   4   5

(7)   The facilitators enabled participants to fully enter into the workshop process.

1   2   3   4   5

(8)   The facilitators listened well to the participants and helped make connections between their insights and the content of the workshop.

1   2   3   4   5

(9)   The facilitators handled questions respectfully and clearly.

1   2   3   4   5

(10) The facilitators helped participants to reflect on their own experience.

1   2   3   4   5

(11) The amount of material presented was just about right.

1   2   3   4   5

(12) The length of the workshop was just about right.

1   2   3   4   5

(13) The amount of reading assigned was just about right.

1   2   3   4   5

(14) There was sufficient time for personal reflection.

1   2   3   4   5

(15) There was adequate opportunity for sharing among participants.

1   2   3   4   5

(16) The workshop enabled me to grasp the ecclesiological, spiritual, and interpersonal components necessary for collaborative ministry.

1   2   3   4   5

(17) The thing I liked best about the workshop was

_____

_____

(18) The thing I liked least about the workshop was

_____

_____

(19) The facilitators' major strength was

_____

_____

(20) The facilitators' major weakness was

_____

_____

(21) The major benefit I received from the workshop was

_____

_____

APPENDIX F

Presentations: Sessions I–V

This appendix provides summaries of each of the five presentations that are vital during the implementation of the workshop. The presentation summaries for Session I, II, III, IV, and V can be further expanded by material in Chapters I, II, III, IV, and V respectively.

Presentation Summary: Session I
An Ecclesiological Foundation for Collaborative Ministry

I *Definition of Collaborative Ministry* [hereafter C.M.]
   —All the baptized are called to holiness, mission, and ministry;
   —C.M. is rooted in the vision of church as communion, where all the baptized are called and gifted; implies availability for service, readiness to dialogue, and fidelity to build up the kingdom of God.

II *The Effects*
   —Our equal status through baptism enables participation in decision-making;
   —No one person or group monopolizes the tasks, initiatives, or policy making;

—Authority = service to promote communion; working in harmony with others; empowering each other; utilizing everyone's expertise.

III *The Challenges*
—Demands trust, maturity, commitment; calls us to communicate honestly/freely; requires we pray together/celebrate eucharist; calls for conversion; build the Lord's kingdom, not our own.

IV *Vatican II: New Insights into Ecclesiology*
—Two images of the church: people of God; communion;
—All are called to be active in mission and ministry and to evangelize society (A.A. 1);
—In baptism all of us share in the priestly, prophetic, and royal priesthood (L.G. 10);
—Lay ministers: mediators between pastor and people of God; active reconciling the lapsed; instructing others on the word of God; work in communion with pastors;
—Pastors: foster co-responsibility with lay ministers (A.G. 21); listen to prudent advice/act upon it.

V *Changing Role of the Pastor*
—Laity expect more: good administration; creative/participatory liturgies; good homilies; effective/personal pastoral care.

VI *Evolving Role of the Laity* (Acts 5:20–24)
—Proclaim the gospel within family; witness at work (G.S. 31, 43, 65, 68, 75); minister to friends;
—Ordained: service of word and sacraments; inclusive of lay ministry (A.A. 6; L.G. 12); laity assist pastors preach more effectively.

VII *Formation for Ministry*
—Keep pace with spiritual/theological progress in the church (A.A. 28); need to be holistic; collaborative in design; provide deeper knowledge of faith; make known the message of Christ (A.A. 31); involve laity and clergy in formation together.

VIII   *1985 Extraordinary Synod:*
  —Promote/celebrate/verify Vatican II; cooperation between clergy/ laity vital (L.G. 10, 26); laity involved in mission of church; active in evangelization of society (G.S. 31, 43, 65, 68, 75);
  —Collaboration: growing participation in decision-making; fidelity to one's baptismal vocation fosters communion (U.R. 6); greater cooperation essential for development of kingdom within the parish (L.G. 10).

 IX   *1987 Synod: The Vocation and the Mission of the Lay Faithful in the Church and in the World*
  —Consultation undertaken in preparation for this synod was extensive; collaboration laity/clergy generated communion;
  —It promoted the equal dignity of women and men; focus on the call to all the baptized to mission and ministry (L.G. 32; C.L. 127); encouraged women's role in the new code of canon law be known and implemented; fostered coordinated presence of women and men in ministry (C.L. 131, 136);
  —Laity: growing consciousness of being baptized into ministry (Doohan, *Grass Roots Pastors,* p. 12);
  —Collaboration between clergy/laity is essential, not an optional extra.

  X   *Conclusion*
  —C.M. has a solid ecclesiological foundation: Vatican II (A.G. 2, 5, 7; L.G. 39, 40); 1985 Synod; 1987 Synod;
  —All are called to build communion with the risen Lord and with each other;
  —Sound faith is necessary for collaborative ministry;
  —Ongoing formation necessary—Vatican II documents; post-conciliar documents;
  —Communion is our point of departure, not of arrival;
  —All ministries need to be evaluated according to how they hinder/develop communion (G.S. 42; L.G. 9, 10, 33; A.A. 27; U.R. 5, 12);
  —Ongoing conversion is essential.

Reflection Questions

(1)   What is my ecclesial vision and how is it evident in my ministry?

(2)   What challenges does collaborative ministry present to us as a pastoral team?

Pope Paul VI: Communio

In a public address on December 9, 1965, Paul VI stated that *communio* speaks of the Christian's incorporation into the life of Christ, and the communication of that life of charity to the entire body of the faithful, in this world and in the next, union with Christ and in Christ, and union among Christians, in the church.

Paul VI, Wednesday General Audience Talk (June 8, 1966): *Insegnamenti* IV, 794 quoted in *Christifideles Laici,* 46–47.

Abbreviations

A.A.   *Apostolicam Actuositatem:* The Decree on the Apostolate of the Laity.

A.G.   *Ad Gentes:* The Decree on the Church's Missionary Activity.

C.L.   *Christifideles Laici:* 1987 Synod on The Vocation of the Lay Faithful in the Church and in the World.

L.G.   *Lumen Gentium:* The Dogmatic Constitution on the Church.

G.S.   *Gaudium et Spes:* Pastoral Constitution on the Church in the Modern World.

S.C.   *Sacrosanctum Concilium:* The Constitution on the Sacred Liturgy.

U.R.   *Unitatis Redintegratio:* The Decree on Ecumenism.

Presentation Summary: Session II
A Spiritual Foundation for Collaborative Ministry

A spirituality that facilitates collaborative ministry is integrated with the ecclesiology of communion:

>—it increases cooperation/co-responsibility in ministry, and focuses on the discovery of Christ's presence in the individual/community.

I *Christ's Presence in Humankind*
  Our dignity stems from: being created in God's image and likeness (Gen 1:26–27);
  >—Irenaeus affirmed: it is necessary to be "grafted" into the word of God in order to live in the image and likeness of God;
  >—Our dignity stems from our relationship with the Trinity;
  >—Scriptures/fathers express the equal dignity of men and women and their ability to communicate with God;
  >—1987 Synod recommended fuller use of the diverse charisms of all the baptized in the mission of the church (L.G. 32; C.L. 127).

Incorporation into Christ's body = church.
Communitarian dimension of being "in Christ" (Col 3:9–11):

>—We are made new (Gal 2:20) implies communion/dialogue/dynamism/ growth until Christ be formed in you (Gal 4:19).

John the evangelist—the indwelling of the Spirit:

>—The believer in Christ/Christ in the believer (Jn 6:56);
>—Bonding between Christ and the individual = vine/branches (Jn 15:5, 7);
>—Clarifies conditions for remaining in Christ: belief in Jesus; fidelity to commandments (1 Jn 3:23–24); love of one another;
>—Pre-eminence to love for God (Mt 22:37);
>—Calls us to mutual love (Lk 10:33);
>—"Beloved, if God has loved us so, we must have the same love for one another" (1 Jn 4:11);
>—Present when two or more gather in his name (Mt 18:20);

—Christ's presence among us = foundation for C.M.

—Our dignity—stems from our relationship with Christ;

—Holy Spirit promotes this dignity/generates communion.

II   *Shared Responsibility for the Mission of the Church*
Pastoral initiatives discerned with Christ present promote: cooperation, mutual respect, and collegiality which increases the commitment of those consulted to implement various goals and objectives.

—The presence of Christ among us: source/summit of C.M.

III   *Conditions for Establishing Christ's Presence*
"Where two or three are gathered in my name, there am I in their midst" (Mt 18:20).

(1)   Athanasius applied to those who are physically separated yet spiritually united;

(2)   Basil: doing the will of God is the condition for establishing Jesus' presence among us;

(3)   Theodore: mutual love = the condition for Christ's presence in the community;

(4)   John Chrysostom: loving others out of love for Christ/laying down one's life as Christ did;

(5)   Peter Chrysologus: "If two of you agree on earth about anything at all for which they ask it shall be done for them."

Some fathers said these conditions for establishing Christ's presence among us are the vocation of the entire church.

—Vatican II: all the baptized are co-responsible for establishing Christ's presence among us (S.C. 7; A.A. 17, 18; U.R. 8);

—The presence of the risen Lord enables us to fulfill our mission, deepens communion, and promotes the sharing of responsibility

IV   *Communion: the Work of God*
God calls us to experience communion with him and with each other:

—Our neighbor is the very means of union with God, not an obstacle to union;

—Communion is promoted by time spent in prayer, reflecting and living out the word of God, celebrating the eucharist together, and reflecting during intense periods of ministry;

—Clergy/laity are called to experience a spiritual communion of goods;

—Communion implies renunciation (1 Cor 9:2);

—Christ crucified is the model for C.M. (Jn 17:23);

—Examining pastoral needs/discerning how to meet them may cause division;

—Pastoral team are co-responsible for evaluating pastoral needs and identifying and resolving the cause of any conflict, which generates trust, promotes a deeper level of sharing, and fosters collaboration.

V   *Living the Word Creates Communion*

The fathers of the church valued the word of God and promoted living it out:

—Clement of Alexandria—must be nourished with the seed of life contained in the Bible in the same way we are nourished with the eucharist;

—Augustine—the proclamation of the word without the testimony of deeds is a scandal to non-Christians today; the one who hears the word of God negligently will be no less guilty than the one who, out of distraction, lets the body of Christ fall to the ground.

Vatican II reinforces the equal importance of the table of the word and the table of the eucharist (D.V. 6, 21);

—Living the word fosters harmony in the community, and makes the eucharist the summit/source of all forms of collaborative ministry (Jn 17:21); and deepens communion (Eph 4:23–24).

Clement of Alexandria: living the word generates Christ's presence in individuals and communities.

—The Word of Life promotes communion and provides cohesion for all programs, ministries and organizations, and fosters C.M. in the parish and promotes evangelization in society.

VI *Role of the Pastor = Spiritual Leader*
(1) To promote the dignity of every member of the community;
(2) To ensure that conditions for establishing Christ's presence (When two or more are gathered . . .—Mt 18:20) are realized;
(3) To encourage all to live the Word of Life and promote the spiritual communion of goods.

The pastor is responsible to the pastoral team for ensuring that all pastoral initiatives are discerned with Christ's presence among the team.

   —The pastor provides a model for the pastoral team by exercising spiritual leadership and promoting communion.

VII *Pastoral Team: Co-Responsible*
   —For recognizing Christ's presence in all;
   —For promoting Christ's presence in every sphere of ministry;
   —For utilizing the various charisms in building up the kingdom.

Reflection Questions

1. When have I experienced the presence of the risen Lord and with whom did I share it?

2. What can I do to ensure that the Lord is always present when we meet as a parish staff?

Presentation Summary: Session III
The Interpersonal Skills and Leadership Styles
That Promote Collaborative Ministry

I *Leadership Styles*
The universal vision of the church is evident in the way that the local church organizes its communal life. Different styles of organization promote collegiality, express the baptismal rights of the people of God, and promote the sharing of responsibility for mission/ministry.

  (i) *Classic Style*
    —Primary purpose = transmit its heritage; maintain the status quo; stick to tried/tested methods; strong sense of security and nostalgia; meet the needs of many.
    —Authority/power—hands of clergy; little empowering of laity; structure = hierarchical; limits spontaneity, vitality and interdependence.

 (ii) *Charismatic/Intuitive Style*
    —Heavily dependent upon the charisma of the pastor and his ecclesial vision;
    —Positive features: openness to initiative, spontaneity; flexible/innovative; appeals to the more liberal;
    —Authority/power—shared among "inner circle"; danger of "in group";
    —Negative: uncertainty about the future; unhealthy dependence on pastor for vision and leadership.

(iii) *Semi-Mutual Style:* emerged in early 1970s
    —Stresses respect/responsibility of all in planning;
    —Authority is shared collectively;
    —Positive: consensus decision-making; may be stressful; generates communion within the group; offers substantial coordination among leaders for a minimum investment of time;
    —Negative: fails to integrate planning with performance; tasks are implemented in isolation; tasks may be assigned to individual lacking competence to implement; individual's plan can conflict with group's;

knowledge of peers is limited; restricts peer review; can produce high level of stress; diminishing performance;

—Needs spiritual, social, on-the-job interaction to strengthen communion.

(iv) *Mutual Style:* emerged in late 1970s

—Interchangability or roles, e.g. retreat team; emphasizes sharing of authority, accountability;

—Leadership is shared; tasks performed collaboratively; team members have on-the-job interaction; integrates wide range of resources, skills, and charisms;

—Positive: collaborative implementation; interdependency deepens trust; observe each other's performance; affirm/provide feedback; deep level of sharing/growth/learning; freedom to be imperfect, vulnerable, struggle/fail/grow;

—Weaknesses: high investment in time spent in planning, mutual supervision, evaluation, feedback and socializing;

—Balance of time spent engaged in pastoral ministry, with time spent in group maintenance;

—Surrender personal autonomy/independence

—Negative: the authority of the group = oppressive? decision by consensus = time consuming/cumbersome; labor intensive in personnel; all facets of ministry are observed/critiqued.

II *Support and Supervision*

Supervised ministry promotes personal formation, professional development, and collaboration in ministry.

(i) *Classic Style*

—Task is assigned; performed in isolation; report given when task completed; supervision = informal/social and is the task of the pastor alone;

(ii) *Semi-Mutual Style*

—Support in discerning objectives/plans; but lacking during implementation; addresses pastoral priorities/not day-to-day tasks;

(iii) *Mutual Style*
—Support/supervision is in-built and ongoing; is available at formal and informal levels; addresses both planning and implementation; yet requires a high investment of time/energy.

III *Feedback and Evaluation*
Feedback reveals strengths, assesses performance, and highlights blind spots in pastoral development.

(i) *Classic Style*
—Only feedback with weight is the pastor's; teams' contribution is superficial; evaluations can be inaccurate, judgmental, given during a chance encounter, coming from an individual's perspective, and often is perceived in a negative light.

(ii) *Semi-Mutual Style*
—Feedback/evaluation is random/inconsistent; limited to planning; implementation in isolation leads to limited consciousness of issues.

(iii) *Mutual Style*
—Feedback/evaluation is integral to the process and is a shared responsibility; much on-the-job interdependency; balance of time in affirmation with time spent engaged in ministry.

IV *Training*

(i) *Classic Style*
—Requires theological and theoretical knowledge focusing on church as institution;
—Focus on skills of pastor presiding/preaching/reconciling/catechizing;
—People: competent/subordinate.

(ii) *Semi-Mutual Style*
—Focus on planning/theological instruction; laity not subordinate to clergy, but competent to clarify objectives, set goals, implement and evaluate programs.

(iii) *Mutual Style*
—Emphasizes personal development; expands interpersonal skills; encourages theological reflection.

V   *Communication and Communion*

Each member of a pastoral team is a leader in his or her own sphere of ministry; the aim of all ministries is to share responsibility for the mission and ministry of the church.

—The decision-making process determines the quality of the final process; the more involvement in discernment, the greater the commitment to implementation.

Communication is fostered by:

—Sharing feelings/experiences/values; involves trust/risk; confidentiality is crucial for communion; when confidentiality is breached, communion suffers;

—All are equally responsible/accountable for reestablishing/building trust; the depth of a relationship = depth of trust.

VI   *Conflict and Confrontation*

Symptoms that negate communion and need to be addressed are defensive behavior, poor communication, hostility, lack of trust.

—Qualities of healthy conflict management: good relationship between the parties; all group members help resolve the crises; those in conflict deal with facts, not motives; the issue is dealt with briefly, and is resolved to the extent that both parties accept the consequences, and no bearing of grudges.

The *quality* of confrontation within the team is an indication of the effectiveness of the group.

VII   *Conclusion*

—Each team selects the leadership style that suits its pastoral needs/mix and match ingredients.

—Aim to choose the operative style that promotes all who are active in ministry; share responsibility for mission, and deepen collegiality and communion.

—Match the operative style of the team with formation for ministry.

Reflection Questions

1. What is my experience of the leadership style operating within our pastoral team?

2. In what ways do I experience and respond to support, supervision, feedback, and evaluation within our pastoral team?

Presentation Summary: Session IV
Reviewing the Mission Statement

I *Definition*
The mission statement outlines what we are called to be and do as a parish; it is intended to express the universal mission of the church. It reveals our ecclesiological vision and our spiritual heritage.

II *Exploring Our Own Mission Statement*
There are three models that are used in the process of formulating a mission statement:

—Model (1) begins with an individual sharing his or her vision with a group such as the pastoral team which then extends consultation to the parish;

—Model (2) begins with the pastoral team, involves all ministries in the consultation, and then explores the input of members at an open parish meeting;

—Model (3) begins with extensive consultation with a large number of small groups; information is then collated to the pastoral team, which then calls a parish assembly.

Identify which process your community used to develop your mission statement.

(1) individual   →   group   → parish
(2) pastoral team →   ministries   → parish
(3) small groups → pastoral team → parish

III *Common Needs Identified in Mission Statements*
A more vital parish; a stronger sense of unity; a greater quality of community life; a deeper faith commitment; greater involvement of all in ministry; concern to minister beyond the parish; greater participation in liturgy; Christian education for all ages; increased financial resources and facilities; integration of different cultures; concern for the youth.

IV *Compare/Contrast Our Mission Statement with Common Needs*
   —Divide up the mission statement into the following three categories: Ecclesial Vision, Spiritual Foundation, and Leadership Style.

Reflection Question

1. What benefit(s) could be derived from reviewing our mission statement?

V *A Method for Reviewing Our Mission Statement*
Problem: Particular → General—it is too restrictive in design, too subjective, and fails to evoke commitment of the pastoral team/pastoral council—co-responsible:
   (1) raise consciousness/all called to mission;
   (2) educate the parish/value/benefits reviewing the mission statement;
Process
   —identify individuals with leadership skills
   —provide training in small group process
   —employ two consultants: a theologian and a specialist in human development;
(i) Formation: three sessions focusing on skills of active listening, conflict management, and communication; three sessions focusing on Vatican II documents: Liturgy/Lay Apostolate; Church/Ecumenism; Church in Modern World/Mission.
(ii) Pastoral team/pastoral council:
   —formation of sharing groups (max no.—ten); each group chooses one of above Vatican II documents;
   —Four sessions: focusing on context; exploration of content; evaluation of mission statement; proposals for ammending mission statement.
(iii) Feedback—pastoral team:
   —All groups have deliberations on each of the above Vatican II documents; pastoral team composes a rough draft.

(iv) Parish meeting:
      —Amend/refine/ratify Mission Statement;
      —Collaborative process: the more people participate, the greater com-
        mitment and ownership of the mission statement.
 (v) Presentation to Parish:
      —Liturgical celebration: public acceptance/dedication/plaque; all are
        called to ministry; all are co-responsible for building up the kingdom.

Reflection Question

1. How can we promote the review of our Mission Statement?

Presentation Summary: Session V
Developing a Parish Pastoral Plan

I   *Definition*
The mission statement expresses the nature of the church as a pilgrim people called to communion and mission; it focuses on key areas of pastoral concern: e.g., word, sacrament, ministry, stewardship; mission to sanctify and evangelize society—as leaven (G.S. 43; A.A. 6).

The pastoral plan expresses how we achieve communion and mission; the aim is to develop the parish into a community of disciples where all actively promote communion (Jn 17:18; 20:21; L.G. 12, 32; G.S. 42).

II   *Exploring Current Pastoral Initiatives*
—What pastoral needs are being addressed at present?
—What programs are the pastoral team currently implementing?
—What pastoral activity is evident in the pastoral council?
—What needs are being addressed by parish organizations?

III   *Common Needs Addressed by Pastoral Planning*
—Creating a more vital/vibrant parish;
—Promoting a stronger sense of unity;
—Evoking greater commitment to faith;
—Empowering all to be active in ministry through: formation/training/ support/evaluation;
—Integrating communion with mission;
—Fostering evangelization in society;
—Utilizing ecumenical resources for projects.
Vatican II documents provide a foundation for pastoral planning:
—L.G.; A.A.; S.C.; A.G.; G.S.; U.R.

IV   *Compare/Contrast Our Pastoral Plan with Common Needs*
Identify the ecclesial vision, spiritual foundation, and leadership style(s) needed for pastoral planning.

Reflection Question

1.   What "perceived need" is not addressed in our pastoral plan?

V   *A Method for Developing a Pastoral Plan*
The faith experience of the parish needs to be nurtured and developed to implement the mission statement.

(i)   Planning, implementing, and evaluating a *Spiritual Formation Week* promotes a renewal of faith.
   —The aim of the formation week is to promote an experience of communion, through theological input, reflection, liturgies, workshops, and faith sharing focusing on the call of all to communion and mission;
   —A search committee with delegates from the pastoral team pastoral council, and parish organizations collaborates in planning, implementing the spiritual formation week;
   —The goals are to identify the perceived spiritual needs, and to discern the gifts needed by a formation team employed to address these needs;
   —The content of the spiritual formation week is discerned by the pastoral team, pastoral council and search committee.

(ii)   *Coordinator of Ministries*
The responsibilities of the coordinator of ministries include:
   —To discern and utilize the gifts of all; identify the perceived needs; provide formation for lay ministers to address these needs; provide a directory of current ministries; create support groups for all ministries; utilize all available spiritual resources within the community.

(iii)   *Small Groups Utilized*
All of the small groups engaged in developing or reviewing the mission statement are again utilized:
   —To meet four times with each group focusing on one area of the mission statement and its respective pastoral application in the planning process;
   —To identify the perceived needs; articulate goals that address these needs; suggest objectives for pastoral development;

—To report findings back to the pastoral team and pastoral council who compile a draft outline of the pastoral plan.

(iv)   *Open Meeting of Parish*

Communication is vital in preparing for this open meeting. Each household is invited to identify unaddressed needs in the parish and report back to the pastoral team and pastoral council.

> —The open meeting is designed to ratify, amend, and review the pastoral plan;
> —The greater the participation in the consultative process, the more people are committed to implementing the pastoral plan.

VI   *Evaluating the Pastoral Plan* (Annually)

A planning committee from a neighboring parish or a consultant from the diocesan curia is responsible for conducting the annual evaluation of the planning process. Critical questions that are addressed include:

> —Are the mission statement and pastoral plan viable and practical?
> —Is it realistic at this time given available resources?
> —How widely known is the mission statement?
> —Does the wider parish share the goals and objectives of the pastoral plan?
> —What major changes have affected the parish during the previous year?
> —Are the pastoral team and pastoral council ministering to the needs of the entire community?
> —In what ways does the parish support all in ministry?

Reflection Questions

1.   What do I need from the other members of the pastoral team to be effective in pastoral planning?

2.   What are the "perceived needs" our pastoral team must address in order to be collaborative in ministry?